The
Comings
of God

PRAYER -- MEDITATION

394
Han

Hanson, Richard Simon

The Coming of God

Library of the
CHRISTIAN CHURCH (DISC'PLES OF CHRIST)
KALAMAZOO, MICHIGAN

Meditations for the Advent Season

The Comings of God

**Richard
Simon Hanson**

AUGSBURG Publishing House • Minneapolis

THE COMINGS OF GOD

Copyright © 1981 Augsburg Publishing House

Library of Congress Catalog Card No. 81-65645

International Standard Book No. 0-8066-1881-7

All rights reserved. No part of this book may be used or reproduced in any manner whatsoever without written permission except in the case of brief quotations embodied in critical articles and reviews. For information address Augsburg Publishing House, 426 South Fifth Street, Minneapolis, Minnesota 55415.

Scripture quotations, unless otherwise noted, are translated by the author. Scripture quotations marked RSV are from the Revised Standard Version of the Bible, copyright 1946, 1952, and 1971 by the Division of Christian Education of the National Council of Churches.

Illustrations by the author.

Manufactured in the United States of America

Contents

THE THIRD CANDLE

THE FOURTH CANDLE

Preface

Advent is about the coming of God. In these 28 meditations I shall seek to lead our thoughts into the many ways of God's coming that are spoken about in the Scriptures of our Christian-Jewish tradition. Because there are 28 of these meditations, you can count back that many days from Christmas Eve and begin on some day prior to the first Sunday in Advent. Allowing a little space for Christmas Eve preparations, that should take you back to the 24th of November. (If you prefer to cut it closer, you can start on the 25th.)

It is an old custom to light four candles in the season of Advent—one in the first week, two in the second, and so on. Or one different candle each week, if you prefer. These candles may be placed in a wreath with a large candle in the center that is called the Christ Candle. That candle is lit on Christmas Eve and Christmas Day.

The other four candles each have a name as well. The first is the Candle of Prophecy. The second is the Candle of Bethlehem. The third is called the Candle of the Shepherds, and the fourth, the Candle of the Angels.

To make a little ritual of these meditations, you can prepare an Advent wreath with candles, light the candle or candles for each week, and read the meditation for the day. In the meditations the Scripture translations, unless otherwise noted, are my own.

God grace your thoughts and your days.

1

The Candle of Prophecy

We light the first candle of the advent wreath. It is called the Candle of Prophecy. We might call it the candle of speech, because the idea of prophecy is the idea that God speaks and that certain keen-eared people hear the speech and relay it to the rest of us. Prophets are people who speak for God. They are people who hear God's speech in our world and then tell the rest of us what they have heard.

And what is this speech of God that they hear? It is the speech of all creation.

I know a daddy who plays this interesting game with his children. "My boy," he says to his son. "My daughter," he says to his girl. "Let's take a walk and see what God is saying today."

So they walk and they look and they listen. "I know, I know," says the girl, "God is saying blue." And she points at the blue of the sky.

"God is saying butterfly too," says the boy as he points to a fluttering set of wings.

"And ladybug," says the girl, "and green in the bush and red in the berry."

"God says dog," responds her brother, "and squirrel up there in the tree."

"God seems to have much to say," says Dad as the three of them join their hands to enjoy it all the more.

The little game is about God's way of talking.

The idea that God speaks is important in the Bible. The Bible begins by telling us how God talks:

> *The earth was formless and void,*
> *with darkness upon the face of the abyss*
> *and the Breath of God hovering over the face of the*
>   *waters.*
> *God said, "Let there be light!"*
> *And there was light.*

The liturgy goes on: "Let there be an expanse in the midst of the waters and let it divide waters from waters" . . . . "Let the waters be gathered to one place beneath the heavens and let dry land appear" . . . . "Let there be lights in the expanse of the heavens" . . . ."Let the waters swarm with living creatures and let birds fly upon the earth" . . . . "Let the earth bring forth creatures." The message of the opening chapter of the Bible is that all of creation is speech of God.

Whenever we speak, our words are but sounds on the wind. We say what we feel or we say what we must; then those who listen must wait to see if our actions will match our words. Only then can the listeners know how much or how little our words might mean. If our talk is big and our performance doesn't match what we say, people soon learn that it doesn't mean much. "He exaggerates," they say. "His talk doesn't amount to much." But we can't accuse God of that. God's speech always amounts to something because God's speech is the deed itself. God's speech is the very events of creation. According to Genesis 1, each day is a sentence of such speech.

A poet who once observed this wrote a psalm that says it well. Its opening lines are these:

> *The heavens declare the glory of God;*
> *the skies display the work of his hands.*
> *Each night pours forth a speech;*
> *each day announces knowledge.*
> *There is not a speech, not a word*
> *but what their voice is heard*   (Ps. 19:1-4).

This is a comforting thought. It means that we are surrounded by speech of God. Another psalmist tells us that we can't get away from God's speech or God's presence even if we try:

> *Where might I hide from your presence?*
> *If I climb to the skies, you are there.*
> *If I lie down in death, there also.*
> *Could I flee on the wings of the wind*
> *and camp far beyond the ocean,*
> *even there your presence would follow,*
> *your strong arm would grasp me*   (Ps. 139:7-10).

There are people who don't know this or feel it. There are people who feel that God is far from us, paying no heed to this creation. Or, perhaps, that there is no God at all.

Prophets are sent for people like that, for the multitudes who do not hear the speech of God or behold the wonders of God's presence. Prophets are persons who use their own eyes and ears for the sake of the many with ears that do not hear and eyes that fail to see.

The Scriptures tell us of many such prophets. In this week of meditations we shall focus on a few—six of them, to be precise. Each will represent a different speech of God by which we and our ancestors in the faith have lived for these many centuries. Each of these will show us a word or a way in which God speaks. By pondering those words and ways, perhaps we shall come to understand that God speaks to us in many ways—not least, through prophets who hear and see and sense God's will.

When we understand these things, let us think of the fact that every prophet needs disciples. The words of the prophets of old and the words of Jesus would not have been written down for further generations if there had been no disciples. Disciples are people faithful to the task of relaying the word to the world around them.

Therefore, if we hear a word that is word of God, it should be a burden upon us to tell it to others. If God is God, God is God of all. Who am I to be selfish about the message that comes to me? If the message is a warning, I should pass on that warning that all might be warned in time. If the message is comfort, then, for the sake of my brothers and sisters, I should share that comfort. If the message is simply the glory of God and creation, I should fearlessly sing that song for all the world to hear. All the world needs such a song, does it not?

Speech is a gift. God's speech is the greatest. My speech can relay God's speech to others.

> *Praise you for speech, for speech of earth and speech of the stars, for words that we speak to each other and, most of all, those words by which you give us the strength, the wisdom, and will to live this day. Praise you for speech that moves our tongues to sing the songs of praise that bravely light our way.*

2

Abraham,
Friend of God

Again we light the first candle, the Candle of Prophecy—
this time in honor of Abraham, friend of God.

How would you like to be known as the friend of God?
That is how Abraham came to be known. So accustomed was
he to conversing with God that his children and grandchildren
called him the friend of God.

They also called him Abraham, which means "Big Daddy."
That is because he was their chief as well as their father and
grandfather. Abraham was the chief of an ancient clan of
shepherds that travelled from Ur of Mesopotamia to the hilly
country of Canaan.

He travelled because God came to him with a message.
God came to the man who was father of us all in the faith, the

father of Christian, Moslem, and Jew. God came as a word
that said

> *Go, you, from your land,*
> *from your birthplace,*
> *the house of your fathers,*
> *to the land that I will show you*   (Gen. 12:1).

When Abraham heard that voice, he lived at the edge of
the city, serving its citizens with milk and cheese, wool, woolen
garments, and the skins of sheep and goats. He and his people
were part of the economy of Ur. They were not, perhaps, full
citizens of the place. The priests and priestesses, who ruled in
the names of the gods and goddesses of Ur, ruled in the center
of the city. The shepherds lived on the outskirts of town.

Out there on the edge of the city Abraham heard that Voice
that said *go,* and Abraham obeyed. Abraham went.

Where did the Voice come from? From within his bosom
or his head? From a fetish that he held in his hand or a set of
sacred dice? No, likely not, for those were the ways that Abraham was to reject. The voice was not a near voice. It was not
a voice from within. It came from the sky above him, for his
God was the God over all other gods, the God of the heavens.

As Abraham left and learned to journey, he came to call
this voice the Voice of the Most High, of the One above all,
the Voice of the All-seeing, the Eternal, the One who Binds
All. Wherever he travelled, he knew this Presence above him.
Wherever he stopped to sojourn for awhile, he made an altar
of earth and stone that in every place he might worship. There,
on those altars of earth and stone, he slaughtered sheep or
goats, poured out the blood as a tribute to the Giver of Life,
burned the fat as an offering, and ate roast meat with his people.
The communion feast was the form of his worship.

The way of faith for our forefather Abraham was to follow
in obedience to the Voice and to pause and enjoy the fruits of
the earth that were given to him. The Voice that spoke to him
from the sky above was none less than that Single Force that

is the Creator of all. The Voice was the source of all that is. Abraham was tuned to that source. He knew it as the source of his own blood and bone and his destiny. He followed it, and that justified his life as a man. It became his *righteousness* or *victory,* says the Scripture, and that in turn became a way of faith for all of us. By listening to the Voice, Abraham became the father of all who believe.

What about us in our place, surrounded by the lights and the smog, and the myriad sounds of our modern cities? Can we possibly hear the sound of the Voice of the Most High? There are times when we scarcely see the sky, let alone hear its commands. When we do, can we feel its embracing unity that holds all on earth within its grasp and connects us with the farthest stars? What is the message of the One who speaks out of space and time? Is it that I too should leave my place and wander the face of the planet? Perhaps. Perhaps not.

What the Voice still says, it seems to me, is that I cannot afford to be tied to one place on this planet, to assume that one culture, one city, one language might be more holy than others. I must be free to experience my kinship with all creatures and all other cultures. As all things are embraced by the blue expanse of the sky, so we are all connected by that same heaven to which we all can look up—if we will.

As he journeyed, Abraham met another like himself. The man was Melchizedek, king of Salem and priest of the Most High God. That man served him bread and wine in the name of that God and pronounced a blessing upon him. Abraham responded with a gift that declared their kinship. To worship the same God is to be brothers in faith.

What richer experience of meeting can we know than this? When two or more who have heard the same Voice come together, in the same moment, they honor each other and the One who Binds All.

Life can be like that. Life should be like that. Our meetings should be discoveries of That which Binds all, Sees all and Speaks to all out of the unity that is eternal.

Praise you for skies above that are the stretch of your arms about me, for the wideness of your word and the message that you will guide us beneath the expanse of your mighty embrace, for the promise and all promises that make it possible for us to believe.

3

Moses and God the Redeemer

Once again we light the first candle. This time in honor of Moses, prophet from the desert of Sinai.

When Israel was in Egypt land,
Let my people go!
Oppressed so hard they could not stand,
Let my people go!
Go down, Moses,
'Way down in Egypt land;
Tell old Pharaoh,
Let my people go.

God came to Moses in a burning bush. He called the name of the man, and the man answered. "Here I am."

"Do not come near," said the Voice from the bush. "Take

off your shoes, for the place where you stand is holy ground. I am the God of your fathers, the God of Abraham, Isaac and Jacob" (Exod. 3:5-6).

What the man Moses heard and saw that day caused him to challenge the mighty god-king of Egypt, the pharaoh. "Let my people go that they may serve their God," said the prophet, and when Pharaoh refused there followed a battle of the gods that became the triumph of the people of Israel. The unseen Fire-voice of the desert and his man Moses struggled against the god-king of Egypt and won.

The arena of battle was the serpentine land of the Nile. Plague after plague, one natural disaster followed another, until finally the young Horus himself, the next god-king of Egypt, lay dead in his bed. In anguish the pharaoh cried out, "Rise up! Go forth from among my people! You and the Israelites—go serve the Lord as you said!" (Exod. 12:31).

Assembled by Moses they left, and that day became the first of the months for those people, to be celebrated as their exodus from Egypt.

Three months later they were assembled in the wilderness of Sinai. There Moses spoke words of importance to them. He spoke for God and his words were these: "You have seen what I did to Egypt, how I picked you up on the wings of eagles and brought you to myself. Now, as surely as you listen to me you will keep my covenant and become my most precious people, though all the earth is mine. You shall be for me a kingdom of priests, a sanctified people" (Exod. 19:4-6).

The coming of God through Moses was a coming for the sake of redemption. It was a time in which God redeemed the people called Israel.

Redeemed? We have almost lost the meaning of that old word. We still use it when we speak of redeeming coupons, bonds, and banknotes. How do we redeem a bond or some coupons? We go to the redemption center with a book of stamps, pick out a toaster, a set of towels or something we want even more. Then we present the book of stamps and take, in exchange, the item we want. The stamps are redeemed, and we are happy because we exchange them for something of value.

The redeeming of people is far more personal than that. To redeem a person is to discover and declare the worth of that person. In the centuries when slavery was common, many a person was redeemed from slavery by being purchased for freedom. A Jewish family, for example, would hear that a certain uncle or cousin had been kidnapped for the slave market. Money would be raised, and the person would be located and purchased. Once purchased he would be a free man again. His dignity as a person was declared by that purchase. His worth was proven by the price. Whatever his family and friends had to pay, they had proved that he was worth that much and more to them. They had proved it by what they had done.

Moses, as prophet of the Lord, was an agent for the redemption of his people. When he challenged the pharaoh with his "Let my people go," he was declaring that they were not to be slaves. They were God's people, and, as God's people, they deserved to be free. Therefore, "with a strong arm and an outstretched hand" God led them out of Egypt. He redeemed them. He declared them worthy of attention, of love, of use. They became a chosen priesthood who would declare the unity of God before all the world as they learned to recite their creed: *Hear, O Israel, the Lord your God is Lord alone.*

Centuries went by. Time and again the people of Israel became slaves to others. At one time they were enslaved by the Romans, and a young woman named Mary became pregnant with child. She was told that this child would be a new hope for her people. She responded by singing a hymn of praise that includes these lines:

> *My soul magnifies the Lord;*
> *and my spirit rejoices in God my Savior,*
> *for he has regarded the lowliness of his handmaiden. . . .*
> *He has shown strength with his arm. . . .*
> *he has put down the mighty . . .*

and exalted those of low degree.
He has helped his servant Israel
in remembrance of his mercy   (Luke 1:47-54 RSV).

This is a hymn about redemption, about God redeeming his people. Once again the people Israel was to be redeemed. Once again they would be known as God's chosen people, and this daughter of their tribes, this Miriam of Nazareth, would be called blessed for the son that she bore.

This is the gospel we inherit. We can call it the Gospel of Redemption. It is the message that God comes to a people to show them that they are worthy of being watched and loved, that they shall be used as instruments of his grace.

The Bible is the story of God's coming to redeem the Hebrews by taking them out of Egypt, through the desert, to a promised land. It is the story of how God led them through the thick and thin of history to make them a light to the nations. In the New Testament it becomes the story of how their Messiah came to redeem them again. Though they were but a fallen nation, he would lift them up. He would make them a blessing to all the world. Their God was God of all nations. By redeeming them, he would redeem all nations. They are shown that each and all are children of God. They are worth the price of the Christ, and with that price they are redeemed.

Praise you for being our Father who comes for all and loves us all with a love that makes us your children, for the message of Moses and the message of Jesus which tell us that we are precious to you, our Creator, our Father, our Friend.

4

The Prophet
and the Earthquake

As we light the first candle of Advent for the fourth time, we light it in honor of a prophet who lived more than 2700 years ago—and in honor of an earthquake that happened in his time.

If you have never experienced an earthquake, you will have to imagine a deep, deep rumbling that seems to come everywhere beneath your feet—like the roaring of a very huge lion that has been lying asleep beneath the ground and just now is waking after a long, long sleep. And then you must imagine the ground and the very mountains beginning to move. Trees are tottering, and the waters of lakes and rivers begin to act strangely as they toss to and fro. Buildings begin to tremble and totter. Cracks appear in walls that were made of stones so huge you might think they would stand forever. But now they crumble and fall to the ground. Huge cracks appear in the earth itself, and fire breaks forth from some of them. It is as though that giant lion is stretching and rising right through the crust of the earth.

The man in whose honor we light this candle was named Amos. There was something strangely keen about him. He began to speak of that earthquake two years before it happened. "The Lord roars out of Zion," he said, and then he went on to talk about the fire breaking forth. People thought he was crazy or just seeing things. But when the earthquake occurred, the people began to realize that Amos was a speaker of truth. They called him a prophet, and we have known him as Amos the prophet ever since.

It is unusual for a man to see something coming before it happens. Most folks don't see things until they happen and even then they don't always see. "Look at the snowflakes coming," says little brother.

"Where are the snowflakes? We don't see any snowflakes," his sisters and parents reply. They think he is wishing for snow so hard that he sees it before it comes.

Now perhaps all that little brother saw was one lone snowflake. But seeing that made him know that more would come, and that is why he cried out, "See the snowflakes coming!" After a while, when many snowflakes have fallen and the ground is white, all the family will have to say, "Little brother was right."

It was something like that for the prophet Amos. He saw terrible things about to happen. He talked about those terrible things to the people of Israel. Because none of them saw those things coming, they didn't believe him at first. But then came the earthquake, and people began to believe him. Some listened to his words. Others wrote them down. Today we have those words in a book of the Bible called the Book of Amos the prophet.

Amos travelled to the city of Bethel to speak to the leaders of the nation of Israel. He knew that those people were blind to the ways of God. He knew that none of them saw the terrible things about to happen. Therefore he went to tell them.

But those people of Israel didn't want to know more than they knew. They thought they knew all they needed to know already. They thought they knew God, and they thought they knew all of God's ways. If there was something they didn't know and needed to know, they simply went to the temple at Bethel to ask the priests. There they performed sacrifices and waited for the answers to their questions and prayers. The priests in their fancy robes would give the answers, and the people were satisfied that those were the answers of God. They had it all figured out—God and religion and the world in which they lived.

Amos the prophet, who was only a simple working man from the village of Tekoa in Judah, knew that they were wrong. He saw the truth that went against their ways. He saw that God is bigger than what people can know or figure out. He saw that God was beyond the control of the priests and too big for the temple in which they worshiped. Amos saw the signs of the great and mighty God in the world around him. If those signs were right, then the people were wrong about God. Amos had to tell them those things.

When Amos talked about God, he talked about one who "forms the mountains and makes the winds and thus declares his ways to man. He brings the dawn out of darkness and treads the heights of the earth" (Amos 4:13). And Amos saw that God was about to do marvelous deeds that would rock the walls of the fortified cities and cause great fires to break out in the capitols of the nations.

The people of Israel did not like the words that Amos was speaking. "Such things cannot be true," they said. "God will not destroy our cities like that. God is kind. God will protect us." Then Amos went on to talk about blight in the fields of grain, and drought and mildew and locust plagues. He knew that the God who provided their food by the gifts of earth and sun and wind and rain would hold back that food for a while. The people had forgotten who God really was. These signs would surely make them turn around and understand those things that they had forgotten.

The leaders of Israel at the temple of Bethel spoke harshly to Amos the prophet. "Get out of this place!" they shouted. "Go back to tending your sheep. Perhaps the sheep will listen to you." Amos responded by calling them fools who would not last long on their thrones of power. He reminded them of things far beyond their control, of things such as earthquakes and mighty winds and the sun and the rain, that God alone can control. In the words he spoke he gave them the signs of God's coming.

In the gospel of Matthew there is a Christmas story that begins with such a sign from God's world of wonders. The sign was a star in God's sky. This star was seen in the east by the magi of the land of Iran. They were wise men, those star-gazing magi—as wise as all who gaze at the stars, the mountains, the rivers, or any of the wonders in God's wonderful world. They were wise because they looked to God's world for signs of God's coming. They followed the star, and that star led them to the bed of a child who was born by God's promise.

If we are wise, we look to God's world of wonders too. We lift our eyes above the skylines of our cities and look beyond the boundaries by which we limit our vision. We look and listen, for out of that world God still speaks with sounds of eternal power that sustain us. The erupting of Mount St. Helens was such a sign for our times. So are the daily risings and settings of the sun, the coming of winter, and the passing of all the seasons. There are millions of signs of God's coming. Some are as large as the mighty sea or the endless sky. Others are as little as the arriving of the first snowflake or the first buds of the spring, or the sway of the palms and the coconut clunking on the ground beneath. All of the sounds and sights and smells of nature are signs of God's coming. Such were the signs for Amos the prophet, and such was the lesson he gave to the world.

Best of all, perhaps, is the miracle of the birth of a baby.

In a cradle made from a manger in Bethlehem, only a few miles from where Amos the prophet once lived, the birth of the baby Jesus was the most powerful sign of all.

Praise you for thunder that signals your power and all disasters of earth that speak through terror to tell of your might, but more especially for gentle forces of fields of snow or tropical nights that tell of your kingdom wrapping itself around the little worlds in which we live.

5

The Prophet Isaiah
and a Sign of Peace

As we light the first candle again, we think of a prophet who saw the presence of the Lord in the coming of a child. The prophet was Isaiah and the child was named Immanuel, which means *God-is-with-us*.

It happened at a time of great national emergency in the history of the Kingdom of Judah. It happened at a time when war was threatening the land. The giant superpower of that time was Assyria, a nation as cruel and greedy as any that has ever been, and the armies of that terrible nation were going farther and farther in their expansion. Every few years they would devour another country that lay in the path of their hunger. Eventually they would control the entire civilized world.

Though it was too late for such a move, two small nations decided to organize other small nations in order to stop the devouring beast. Rezin, the king of Syria, and Pekah, the king of Israel, announced the forming of a coalition. They especially wanted the skillful army of Judah in their train.

Ahaz was king of Judah. He considered it the better part of wisdom to refuse the invitation to join with the kings of Syria and Israel against the Assyrian armies. A similar plan had worked in times past with limited success. Such a plan now seemed like suicide.

But when King Ahaz said no to the request of Israel and Syria, the kings of those two countries declared war on him and promised to put another man on the throne in his place. Ahaz was understandably frightened. "His heart and the heart of his people shook as the trees of the forest shake before the wind" (Isa. 7:2 RSV).

The king went out to inspect the city's water works, wondering whether Jerusalem could hold out for any length of military siege. He was at the end of the conduit at the upper pool on the highway to the fuller's field when he was met by the prophet Isaiah.

"Take heed: relax and do not be afraid," said the prophet. "Don't let your heart faint because of those two smoldering fire-stumps—the wrathful Rezin of Syria and son of Remaliah." Then the prophet spoke a promise to the king of Judah. The promise was this:

> *It shall not happen, it shall not be,*
> *for the head of Syria is only Damascus*
> *and the head of Damascus is Rezin.*
> *The head of Ephraim is only Samaria,*
> *and the head of Samaria, Remaliah's son.*
> *If you do not trust*
> *you will not be trustworthy* (Isa. 7:7-9).

What did the prophet mean? He meant that the heads of kingdoms and leaders of nations are not as mighty as they make themselves sound. Both Syria, with its capital in Damascus, and Israel with its capital of Samaria in the midst of the territory of Ephraim, did not amount to as much as the boasting of their kings. The prophet knew something that is found in some of the psalms.

> *The Lord changes the will of nations*
> *and hinders the plans of peoples.*
> *The king is not saved by great armies*
> *nor the hero spared by great strength.*
> *The Lord's eye is on those who fear him,*
> *who hope in His kindness,*
> *to deliver their lives from death*
> *and revive them in famine*   (Ps. 33:10, 16, 18-19).

But King Ahaz was not up to such faith. He continued to fear and to act in fear. The prophet went on. "Ask a sign of the Lord your God," he said. "Let it be deep as hell or high as heaven."

The king answered, "I will not ask. I will not test the Lord."

"Listen then, House of David," the prophet continued. "Is it not enough that you try the patience of men? Will you try God's patience too? The Lord will give you a sign all the same. Behold, a young woman shall conceive, bear a son, and call his name Immanuel. He shall eat curds and honey when he is old enough to choose between evil and good. And before the child knows how to refuse the evil and choose the good, the land whose two kings you fear will be deserted" (Isa. 7:13-16).

The words were both frightening and comforting. The desertion in the lands of kings Rezin and Pekah was a dire pronouncement of doom. Before the child would reach the age of puberty, the mighty Assyrians would be upon them. And that is precisely what happened. The times were times of disaster, and nothing could avert it. Yet, in the midst of that disaster, hope took the form of a child, the beginning of the next generation. The child was therefore named Immanuel. He was *God-with-us.*

Who was this child? Was he the prophet's son or the son of the king? Or does it matter? Perhaps it is important to know that he was chiefly the son of the young woman who conceived.

And it is important to notice that he was to be a child of peace who would eat curds and honey when he came of age.

Time went on. Time became centuries as kingdoms waxed and waned and king after king went to the dust to sleep with his fathers. Having been subject to Assyrians, Babylonians, Persians and Greeks, the descendants of the people of Judah were subject to new conquerors. Romans came to rule where Assyrian armies had once marched in cruel conquest. Another young woman conceived and gave birth to a son. The woman was named Mary, and the son was named Jesus. It was announced at his birth that he would be a child of peace for peace on earth to men of good will.

The evangelist Matthew made a powerful comment about this child. Thinking back to the time of the prophet Isaiah, Matthew announced that this child truly fulfilled what was spoken by that prophet when he said, "A virgin shall conceive and bear a son and his name shall be called Immanuel" (Matt. 1:23 RSV). The birth of a child in the time of the Assyrian crisis had been the sign of God's presence. The birth of this child, Jesus, in the midst of Roman rule would be the same sign. The child of Mary would be the presence of God in our world. He would be the Prince of Peace.

Praise you for the sign of Immanuel and all other signs of your presence, for the birth of all babies among us as the promise of life going on despite our wars and our foolish behavior as we bow to kings and dictators when we should bow at the cradles of children.

6

The Coming
of the Messiah

Once more we light the first candle, this time in honor of a
prophet who saw the coming of the Lord in the coming of a
king. He saw it in a vision that fed his people with much hope.

> *Rejoice greatly, O daughter of Zion!*
> *Shout loudly, daughter of Jerusalem!*
> *Behold, your king is coming to you!*
> *Triumphant and victorious, he,*
> *humble, riding upon an ass,*
> *on a colt, the foal of a donkey.*
> *I will remove the chariot from Ephraim*
> *and the war horse from Jerusalem.*
> *The battle bow shall be broken*
> *and he will order peace for the nations.*

His dominion shall be from sea to sea,
from the River to the ends of the earth (Zech. 9:9-10).

The vision sounds like a parade on Palm Sunday, for these are the words that people remembered when Jesus rode into Jerusalem on the back of a donkey. That's not accidental, of course. When he rode on the back of the donkey that day, Jesus intended to act out these words.

The story about these words, however, goes back to a time before Jesus. It goes back to times when his people lived in the hope of having their own king—a king such as David or King Hezekiah or King Josiah.

In those days it was not unusual for people to place their hopes in a king. The people of most nations did that. It was not unusual to think that the king was chosen by God. The people of most nations thought that way about their kings.

It was unusual and important, however, that this king should be lowly, that he should ride on a donkey, and remove the war horse from his city. It was important that he would speak peace to his people and peace to all nations. The king would be king of the world, and he would bring peace on earth.

Time went by, as it does. Again and again, Jewish people looked for that king. Would he come soon or late? Would he come at all? Was the hope a vain hope?

Then one day he came, but only as a king for the moment. He was the prophet from Nazareth. He was a man of words, not a man of royal regalia. Yet as king he paraded into the chief city of his people, the city of King David. Lowly he came, on the back of an ass, and the crowds shouted, "Hosanna, Son of David! Blessed is he who comes in the name of the Lord!" (Matt. 21:9).

Some leading men of the city were disturbed. "Teacher, rebuke your disciples," they said. Perhaps they feared reprisal from the Roman authorities for such a riotous demonstration. Or perhaps they feared outright insurrection itself—insurrection that would become the war that might be the end of their nation. For such reasons they objected to what was done. But the prophet replied, "I tell you, if these were silent the very stones would cry out" (Luke 19:40).

One week later, according to the accounts, the prophet stood before the Roman procurator on the charge of having made himself king. According to one witness, the conversation went like this (John 18:33-38):

PILATE: Are you the king of the Jews?

JESUS: Do you say this of your own accord, or did others say it to you about me?

PILATE: Am I a Jew? Your own nation and the chief priests of your temple have handed you over to me; what have you done?

JESUS: My kingship is not of this world; if my kingship were of this world, my servants would fight that I might not be handed over.

PILATE: So you are a king?

JESUS: You say that I am a king. For this I was born, for this I have come into the world: to bear witness to the truth. Every one who is of the truth hears my voice.

PILATE: What is truth?

It was not long before many were proclaiming that this truth-bearer was the awaited Messiah, the King of the Jews and the Jewish king for the world. Not in any normal way, of course, for he was dead and risen. His presence had become the presence of the Spirit of God. The proclamation went forth, and brave missionaries carried it from one land to another. The claim is now familiar to Christians around the globe, where believers in many tongues hail the power of Jesus' name and crown him Lord of All.

Yet the world still waits for peace. The battle bow is not broken. It has only been replaced by the gun, the gas, the missile, and the awful bomb. The battle horse has only given way to armored vehicles, warships, and planes. We seem to be as far from peace on earth as ever we were in the past. Indeed, our century has seen more deadly deeds of war than any other. What can match the atrocities of our time for dimension or lasting effect?

We still wait for peace. Will Jesus of Nazareth be the one who brings it?

Perhaps he also waits. He was, after all, a genuine man of peace. He taught the way of peace to all who followed and learned from him. He taught the kind of love that heals through deeds of mercy. He taught forgiveness, without which the cruelties of the past cannot be resolved. He taught the way that he called the truth. He claimed to be that way and that truth through which we can behold our one true Father. Perhaps he still waits for us to learn that way.

A Palestinian friend of mine spoke one day of the need for peace in the Middle East. He was a Moslem, but he knew something of this way of Jesus. In a moment of anguished thoughts he blurted out, "There should be no war in this land, for this is the land of Jesus!"

It is now ten years since I heard him speak that simple but powerful sentence. It stays with me as an important thing to say. In my own mind I have enlarged it to fit my Christian understanding of the vision of Zechariah. "Should there not be peace in all the earth," I say to myself, "for it is all the land of the Lord?"

For whom does peace wait? For the Messiah to come again? For another? Or does it wait for the followers to truly follow the way that was set before them? The message has come. The man with that message on his lips was among us. Must he come again to establish that peace, or does he wait for us to do our part?

> *Praise you for Jesus, for what he was and what he became, for all that he dared to be in his time to foe and to friend and for all that he beckons us to be in a life that is daring and never dull.*

7

John and the Coming of the Lord

For the last time we light this first candle of Advent alone, the Candle of Prophecy. This time it is for certain prophetic words that we always associate with Advent. They are the words that we find in the 40th chapter of the Book of Isaiah:

A voice cries:
Prepare in the wilderness a way for the Lord!
Straighten the highway in the desert for our God!
Let every valley be raised,
every mountain and hill be lowered
that the uneven ground may be level
and the rough land a plain,
and the glory of the Lord will be revealed.
All flesh will see it together.

These words tell us to prepare for the coming of the Lord. They are the central theme of Advent.

How do we prepare for the coming of the Lord? Do we do it by trying to figure out just when he shall come? Do we do it, perhaps, by baking cookies and fruit cakes and shopping for gifts? Or do we do it by preparing and practicing Christmas programs?

What if we should fail to prepare? What if we do nothing or decide that there is nothing we can do to prepare for the coming of the Lord? Will he come all the same, or might we miss his coming?

We could take the words of the text literally. They speak of a way in the wilderness, of a highway going through the desert. We could therefore envision huge earth-moving machines and the other impressive equipment of road-building crews carving a highway that stretches straight over hills and valleys. And then we could wonder why such violence should be done to the natural terrain for the coming of the Lord. We have done such things for the coming of earthly kings, of course. We have laid out pavements and carpets so that their dignified feet need not touch the bare earth. But this one is Lord of nature. This one is nature's Creator and Friend. Are not the rough places the best of highways for him?

The words are metaphors. To take them literally is to miss what they mean. Therefore let us listen to one who explained how they are to be taken. Let us listen to the prophet John, who appeared on the banks of the Jordan river some six centuries after those words were first spoken.

John wore a garment of camel's hair, we read in the Gospel of Matthew, and a leather girdle around his waist. He ate the natural foods of the wilderness and deliberately lived out there where the ground was rough and the topography anything but plain. He spoke stingingly harsh words of judgment in which he demanded correction in the lives of those who came to hear him. "You brood of vipers! Who warned you to flee from the wrath to come? Bear fruits that signify turning and do not be so presumptuous as to say to yourselves, 'We have Abraham as our father.' I tell you, God is able to raise up children for Abraham from these stones. Even now the axe is laid to the root of the trees. Every tree that bears no good fruit is cut down and thrown to the fire" (Luke 3:7-9).

He was questioned by some. "Who are you?" they asked. "Are you trying to be the Messiah?"

"Not the Messiah," said he, "for that One is greater than I and he must come after me."

"Are you, then, the prophet Elijah come back? Are you the prophet?"

"No," said John. "I am the voice that cries in the wilderness, 'Prepare the way of the Lord!' " Then he went on to quote that entire passage from the Book of Isaiah.

John came preaching repentance and forgiveness of sins. He taught people to share what they had with each other, to be fair, and to undo the wrongs of the past. He taught people to turn to the Kingdom of God that was at hand. They should turn to behold the glory of the Lord that would be revealed. They should turn from their greed and the fears that produced that greed to the coming of their God. Thus they could prepare the way of the Lord.

The rough and crooked places that needed to be levelled and straightened were the places inside them. They were crooks, to put it as bluntly as John. They needed to be reformed at least enough to see the Lord's coming. They were dirty with the dirt of sin. They needed to be washed. Therefore John washed them in the water of the Jordan River. The Greek word for washing was *baptism*.

There is a grand old American hymn that puts these thoughts into metrical words. It is about the judgment that accompanies and precedes the coming of the Lord. Harriet Beecher Stowe wrote the words:

Mine eyes have seen the glory of the coming of the Lord.
He is trampling out the vintage

Where the grapes of wrath are stored.
He has loosed the fateful lightning of his terrible swift
*   sword.*
His truth is marching on.
Glory, glory, hallelujah!
His truth is marching on.

It fits. It fits the career of John the Baptist and the careers of prophets before him. It fits this season of Advent in which we seek to be turned toward the coming of God and of his Christ. We need to prepare, do we not, as much as the people of Jesus' day? We need to turn that we may behold God's glory.

Who shall turn us?

Do we have in our time prophets like John who can show us the crookedness of our ways that they may be straightened? Perhaps we do. If so, we should listen to them. But if we do not, let us listen again to John. Let us turn from greed and lying. Let us turn from the ways that lead to violence and war. Let us turn to sharing and kindness, to the deeds that lead to peace. We are best prepared for the coming of the Lord when we are found doing those works which he has commanded.

> *Praise you for voices that shake our senses and words that turn us from pride and greed and the busy little deeds of our busy little worlds in order that we may desire your coming and desire the ways of peace.*
> *Praise you for cleansing judgments and baptisms that renew us and all fires that burn the film from our eyes that we may behold the glory that beams forth from the manger bed of Bethlehem.*

8

The Candle
of Bethlehem

As we light the second candle of Advent, we light the Candle of Bethlehem.

Not many great cities are as well-known as this little old town of Bethlehem. How many of them have candles lit in their honor? To how many of them do we sing songs as lovely as this Christmas carol?

> *O little town of Bethlehem, how still we see thee lie.*
> *Above thy deep and dreamless sleep the silent stars go by.*
> *Yet in thy dark streets shineth the everlasting light.*
> *The hopes and fears of all the years are met in thee*
> *   tonight.*

The Bible contains many stories about Bethlehem. The birth of Jesus is only one of many things that happened in that place.

There is the story of the Levite who left Bethlehem and wandered north to find employment in the home of Micah until the clan of Dan took him away and made him priest of their tribe in the north, at the sanctuary of their city of Dan. This story is found in the Book of Judges, Chapters 17-18.

There is the terrible story of another Levite who lived in the highlands of Ephraim and went to Bethlehem to hire a servant girl. She went with him to his home in Ephraim, but he treated her so badly that she ran away and returned to her father's home in Bethlehem. The Levite came after her and took her again. On his way back to Ephraim he stopped for the night in the Benjaminite city of Gibeah. There he was bothered by some local hoods. To protect himself he gave them his servant girl for a night of fun. They raped her so many times that by morning she lay dead at the door of the house where her master slept. This story is also found in the Book of Judges, in Chapter 19.

The lovely story of the Book of Ruth takes place in Bethlehem.

Most important of all, Bethlehem is the home town of the lad who became the great king David, the lad who was great-grandson of Ruth. This made Bethlehem the family home of all who would be Messiah.

Bethlehem was the home of the heroes Asahel and Elhanan, two of David's famous thirty champions.

Later in time, when patriotic Jews of Jerusalem murdered governor Gedaliah to protect the Babylonian rule of their city, they stopped there before fleeing for safety to Egypt. This story is found in the Book of Jeremiah (41:17). In the books of Ezra (2:21) and Nehemiah (7:26) we learn that many of the citizens of Bethlehem were taken as exiles to Babylon.

Most important of all for Christians, this village was the birthplace of Jesus.

Through this week we shall think about the comings of God to Bethlehem and such comings as are common to other cities and villages of our world. It is in the villages and cities that most people live. If God does not come to villages and cities, then most of earth's people shall be abandoned to themselves.

Yet it is in our cities that we humans fight our biggest battles against God's coming. We fight God there in a thousand ways. It is there that we make up the rules that sometimes go against the rules of God's world. It is there that our greed most gets us in trouble. It is from our cities that we rob the earth of its treasures and pour back pollution. It is there in our cities, where we gang up together as mortals, that we seem to go most against nature and God.

It is important, therefore, to know that God comes to our cities. And how does God come? Or how do we know of his coming, and what can we do to welcome him there? We are surely not able to keep God out of our cities, but are we able to welcome him there?

When Mary and Joseph sought a room for the night in Bethlehem, there was no place in the inn. That did not stop the coming of the child. Mary and Joseph were directed to the stables, and there, with the warmth of the animals for heat and where nature ruled the simple beasts, the son of Mary was born. Room or no room in the inn, the Christ child came.

Perhaps God comes even though we try to stop him.

Praise you for coming, for coming to mangers in stables, to slums and street corners, to bedrooms and kitchens, and all such ordinary places where we live life or labor and learn as our days move on to the last great coming of our lives.

9

The Story of Ruth

One of the oldest stories about Bethlehem is the story of Ruth, Naomi, and Boaz. As the story begins, the family of a man named Elimelech was forced to leave the village of Bethlehem because of a famine there. Now a famine in Bethlehem was hardly proper, for the name Beth-lehem means "house of bread." To say that there was a famine in Bethlehem was to say that there was no longer any bread there in the house of bread.

Elimelech migrated east to Moab with his wife Naomi and his two sons. There the sons married Moabite women. But alas, both father and the two sons soon died, and the three women were left without husbands—Naomi the mother and her two daughters-in-law, Ruth and Orpah.

Then came the line in the story, "She started with her

daughter-in-law, Ruth, to return from the country of Moab. For she had heard in the country of Moab that the Lord had visited his people to give them bread" (Ruth 1:6). Once again the House-of-Bread was provided with bread! Why? Because the Lord had visited his people. The coming of God meant the coming of bread.

It is always that way. God comes with sun and rain and good weather, and we are all fed. God is the One who provides what we eat. No matter that we go to a market to get it. No matter that it comes to our table from a kitchen. At the beginning of the process, out in the farmers' fields, God is the One who gives us bread. That is why we pray to God when we pray for daily bread.

There are ancient psalms that tell us about it in lovely ways. Some of the loveliest lines come from Psalm 65:

> *The cycles of morning and evening sing out.*
> *You have visited the earth and watered it,*
> *you make it abundantly rich.*
> *The rain trough of God is full of water!*
> *You give root to the grain, for so you create it*
> (Ps. 65:9-10).

Psalm 104 has similarly eloquent lines:

> *They all depend upon you*
> *to give them their food in due time.*
> *You give it, for they do but gather.*
> *You open your hand, they have plenty;*
> *you withhold your presence, they are anxious.*
> (Ps. 104:27-29).

It is easy to forget the truth of this. In a world of supermarkets and drive-ins it is easy to forget where food comes from. If we don't look beyond the counter or the grocery shelf when we buy our daily bread, we may not realize that God is still the real giver of life. We may not realize that life is a gift and that all those things that keep life going are gifts as well—

food, water, the air that we breathe. And when we do not understand that these are gifts, then we no longer pause to give thanks
before we eat. Failing to give thanks is a sign of our growing
separation from the Lord of all nature, who is the source of
our life.

Table grace can still be an important token of what we believe. Pausing to recognize the gift and the giver is a way of
recognizing the coming of God in our daily lives. God is unseen, of course. God never comes as totally God to be seen by
our eyes. It is in the gifts alone, the gifts that we see or hear or
taste, that we know his coming.

When Jewish people recite a blessing before the meal, they
often use this little prayer that recognizes the coming of God
through bread:

> *Blessed are you, O Lord our God, Ruler of the world,*
> *for you bring forth the bread from the earth.*

To recite this is to believe that God still visits us by giving
bread just as the story of Ruth says.

A table prayer more familiar to Christians is this one:

> *Come, Lord Jesus, be our guest*
> *and let these gifts to us be blest.*

There is something backward about this prayer. It speaks as
though we are the hosts and Christ is the guest. The truth of
the matter is quite the reverse. As truly in our meals as in the
great Communion service we celebrate in our churches, Christ
is the host, and we are the guests. He is the provider, and we
are the ones provided for. According to the Gospel of John,
he was truly the Bread of Life. That is why we read these
words about him:

> *After supper he took the bread,*
> *broke it and gave it to them saying,*
> *"Take it. Eat it. This is my body"*   (Matt. 26:26).

What simple eloquence! He, who had no possessions to his

name, looked about for the signs by which he might be known and remembered for all ages to come. "What am I?" he must have thought to himself. "What is my essence? What can best represent what I mean to be?" Then he seized on the bread—and the wine—and gave that as himself.

We have made a sacrament of that act, and that is most fitting. But should not every act of eating be sacramental? Is not the Lord in all bread that we eat? Is it not God who comes with the gift of life in every loaf of bread—or in the water we drink and the air that we breathe? These things are all the signs of God's coming. By these things we live through each day.

The line in the Book of Ruth goes like this: "God visited his people to give them bread." Perhaps we could change it a bit and say something like this each time we pause to eat: "God has visited to give us bread."

> *Praise you for giving and being yourself in the gift, for giving and being our daily bread, our water of life and the breath that blows the winds of heaven into our lungs to keep us alive and rejoicing.*

10

David the Messiah and Messiah Son of David

The names of King David and Bethlehem go together like peas and pods or comics in Sunday papers. It was from Bethlehem he came, and because of that Bethlehem became known as the birthplace of Judah's kings forever. Visiting Bethlehem as the birthplace of the Messiah has become a pilgrimage for Jews and Christians alike.

Do we know the story of how God came to that lad in Bethlehem to make him Judah's first king?

The tribes of Israel were distressed because powerful enemies hemmed them in on every side. The Philistines, those enemies were called, and those were the days when Samuel was prophet and priest in the land. As for the Israelites and the tribe of Judah, they were a crude lot of shepherds and farmers who could not hold their own against enemies who were organized into armies and equipped with the finest weapons of the day. Clubs and slings were their only weapons, except for an occasional bow or dagger. As is true of primitive folks today, they were the victims of the ambitions of their civilized neighbors.

Finally they became so desperate that they went to the old prophet-priest Samuel to ask for a powerful leader. "Give us a king to govern us," they said (1 Sam. 8:6).

Samuel was not pleased with their request. "Do you really want a king?" he replied. "Do you know the ways of a king? He will recruit your young men and women into his service. They shall serve in his armies and work in his palace courts. Much of your land shall become his land as the king takes more and more for himself and his government officials. Be satisfied that God is your king. That is enough."

But the people were too desperate to be so easily put off. They continued to insist that they needed a king. Samuel prayed to God for guidance and finally conceded that in this case the will of the people was the will of God. He chose the tall warrior named Saul to be their leader, and Saul commanded the armies of Israel for many years.

Saul was not fully a king, nor was he always successful as warrior chief. The old prophet-priest came to understand that he must choose another in his place. It was then that he visited Bethlehem.

He went to the home of Jesse, a shepherd who had eight sons, carrying an animal horn filled with anointing oil. He slaughtered a heifer to make a feast and entertained Jesse as honored guest. As they feasted, old Samuel spoke a blessing of consecration over the shepherd and all his sons. Then he began to study those sons to see which one might be a fitting king for the people. One by one he called them to stand and walk before him. Seven sons passed his gaze, and none seemed to be the one. "Are all your sons here?" asked the prophet.

"The youngest is not. He is out guarding the sheep."

"Send and fetch him. We shall wait till he comes."

David came in from the fields, and when Samuel laid eyes on him, he knew that this was the lad who would be the first king of Judah and all the tribes of Israel as well. He was ruddy and handsome and bright. As the lad knelt before him, the old prophet poured the oil over his head in the primitive ceremony of anointing. Years later, after the tragic death of Saul on the slopes of Gilboa, this lad would become a man and a king.

When David was anointed he became *messiah,* which means "anointed one." The Greek word for that is *Christos* and we have shortened that to *Christ.* "Christ" simply means "anointed one," a title that the Hebrews of old used for a king.

When Jewish people look for the coming of the Messiah, they look for one who must come from the line of David. Like David he must shepherd his people. When Christians speak of Christ, they should think in a similar way. They should think of a shepherd from Bethlehem.

To say that the Christ comes from Bethlehem is to say that he comes from a humble but ancient place. To say that he is Christ is to say that he is chosen—chosen and anointed by the command and the coming of God. And in a strange and mysterious twist of understanding, the coming of that anointed one himself can be the coming of God. There is a psalm about that with these lines:

> *The Lord says to my lord,*
> *"Sit at my right side*
> *til I set your foes down*
> *as a stool for your feet"*   (Ps. 110:1).

This psalm goes on to tell how this Messiah shall rule over those who resist his rule and yet be like the gentle, life-giving dew that appears on the fields at dawn. Like a mortal man he shall drink from humble waterbrooks, but with power that only God can give he shall lift his head high as a king and rule.

When Jewish people of old felt that their Anointed One was coming they shouted "Hosanna" (God save us!). "Blessed is he who comes in the name of the Lord!" That is what some of them shouted one day when Jesus came riding into Jerusalem on the back of a donkey. As they saw him coming, they saw his coming as the coming of God to save them.

This means that God can come in the disguise of a king.

Praise you for parades that permit us to sing of glory and shout hosannas and be stirred by the sights and the sounds of your coming by which you show us that you are still the ruler of all and that the king whom you appoint is one who comes to bring peace.

11

Micah and the Little Town of Bethlehem

Sometimes bad times can help us see good times. When all is distressful and we seem to be walking in darkness, a little bit of light, a slim ray of hope, seems to shine clearer than ever.

Today we shall think about a time like that. A time long ago, to be sure, but a time when the little town of Bethlehem provided a vision of hope for the world. It was a time of distress and war, a time when one mighty nation was conquering all others, a time when people feared the marching of armies and the burning of cities.

The nation that brought on all that fear was ancient Assyria. The Assyrians were so greedy and cruel that they decided to conquer all others. They used the tactic of terror. If another nation did not surrender to their demands, they would choose one of its cities for an example, invade it with an overwhelming force of soldiers and engines of siege, and finally, when that city crumbled before their assault, they would punish the survivors with rape, destruction, and torture. Pregnant women were ripped open at the belly with swords, and their unborn babies were destroyed. The defending soldiers who had bravely resisted would be skinned alive, dismembered, and dragged through the streets, then stuck up on stakes as a wall of rotting corpses to keep guard over the ruins of the fallen city. As they invaded one nation after another, fear of them increased until some surrendered at the first appearance of their armies.

Israel, the Hebrew kingdom of the North, had already succumbed to their onslaught. Micah, a prophet to the kingdom of the South, the kingdom of Judah, felt the threat of their coming. But in the midst of that threat he spoke strong words of confidence. These are his words:

You, O Bethlehem of Ephrathah,
though little among Judah's clans,
from you there will come for me
one to be a ruler in Israel.
His origins are ancient,
from days of long ago.
So, we will give them up
til the time when the woman gives birth.
Then the rest of his brothers will return
and Israel's sons will ascend.
He shall stand as a shepherd in the strength of the Lord,
in the majesty of the name of the Lord, his God.
They are settling down,
for now he has grown,
as far as the ends of the earth
and that shall be peace.
Indeed, the Assyrians enter our land,
they march right into our towns.
But we shall raise up
seven shepherds against them,

yes, eight human princes,
and they shall shepherd the land of Assyria with a sword,
the land of the hunter with shining blade.
They shall deliver from Assyria
when Assyria enters our land
and marches within our borders   (Mic. 5:1-5).

How could the little town of Bethlehem be such a bastion of hope against the armed might of great and terrible Assyria? It would be like expecting Nicaragua to rescue the world from the Soviet Union. How could one prince out of Bethlehem shepherd the Assyrians like a flock of sheep? Was the eighth son David and therefore the one who could do it? David had been dead for more than 150 years.

But no, David was not really dead. The way those ancient Hebrews thought about life and death and descendancy, David lived on in his sons, his grandsons, and on down the line. And David's descendants were the presence of the Lord's authority among the people of Judah. That is why the prophet could say he would rule in the strength of the Lord, in the majesty of the name of the Lord his God.

Christians have inherited that faith—the faith that the Anointed One comes and rules in the strength of our God. Christians believe that the coming of the Messiah is the coming of God.

Is it a coming that was once upon a time—or once upon a time and then once again? Perhaps it is a coming that is more often than that, as often as every time the message of the Messiah is remembered and proclaimed.

Jewish people of old may have looked to every descendant of David with that kind of hope. There are many psalms that show it. The opening lines of Psalm 72 are an example:

Give to the king your justice, O God,
and to the king's son give your victorious goodness,
that he may judge your people rightly,
your poor folk with justice.
Let the hills produce peace for the people,

the mountains, prevailing goodness,
that he may defend the poor
and deliver the needy
and crush the oppressor (Ps. 72:1-4).

To the prophets and to the psalmists, the coming of every anointed son out of Bethlehem was the best hope for the coming of peace. The prophet saw that his people would settle down in peace as far as "the ends of the earth." In the psalm the poet sings these lines:

May he have dominion from sea to sea,
and from the River to the ends of the earth!
May his foes bow down before him,
and his enemies lick the dust (Ps. 72:8-9 RSV).

Their hope in the Messiah was a hope for peace, and Micah the prophet became famous for his vision of peace. Here are some of the lines from that vision:

They shall beat their swords into plowshares
and their spears into pruning hooks.
Nation shall not lift sword against nation,
and never again will they train for war (Mic. 4:3).

And one of those who recorded the message of Jesus as Messiah also recorded a song about peace that was sung by the angels when he was born:

Glory to God in the highest
and peace on earth
among men who know his good will! (Luke 2:14).

Praise you for peace and for all hopes of peace in our world which is filled with wars and rumors of wars. Praise you for visions of light that shine in our darkness and for the all goodness that comes in the midst of our fear and our evil.

12

The Water of Bethlehem

Today let us think about water and about being thirsty—as thirsty as after a long, long run or a day of work beneath the sun, thirsty as if we had not been able to drink for a day or two or three and then we come to a mountain stream where the water is free and flows from the melting snows above, fresh and pure and abundant. How would it feel to drink after such a thirst? Would it not be like a gift of sustaining love?

There is a story about the well at Bethlehem and how the great warrior David, who became King David, treasured the water of that well. But before we hear the story we ought to know something about wells of water in the Middle East where David lived. That land was a dry land where rains came only one half of the year. Because of that, the ancient Hebrews were people who knew how precious water can be.

In the Hebrew language the word for a blessing and a word for a pool of water are almost the same. In the plural form they are identical. Both words come from a word root that signifies kneeling. One kneels to receive a blessing, and one kneels, as well, to drink from a pool of water.

There are hundreds of lovely lines in the Bible about the gift of water. Some are gentle lines, such as the line about the good shepherd leading his flocks beside pools of still water. Others are exciting shouts of praise for the gift of rain. An especially exciting line is found in Psalm 29:

The Lord's voice is over the water.
The majestic God thunders,
the Lord over waters primeval.

But back to the story found in Chapter 23 of the Second Book of Samuel.

David and his warriors had been engaged in a lengthy struggle against the Philistines, who were at that time occupying the village of Bethlehem. David's troops were camped at the Cave of Adullam some 15 miles away. David, the young handsome leader of this outlaw band, was thinking sadly about the fact that Bethlehem was occupied by the Philistine troops. Then he began to think about the well that supplied his home town with water. All of a sudden he expressed his feelings by blurting out, "O that someone would give me a drink from the well of Bethlehem, the well that is near the gate!"

Some of David's men heard the remark and took it as a personal challenge. Three of them sneaked away and travelled on foot all the way to David's hometown. There they broke through the Philistine lines and got to the well. They hastily filled a goatskin with water and made their way back through the enemy lines. Swiftly they ran to escape Philistine arrows and then slowed down to cover the rest of the distance.

When they entered the camp of David with the precious gift of water from Bethlehem, there was a shout of amazed admiration. Who would have dared such a deed? David was overwhelmed by their kindness and their bravery. As he lifted the skin to his lips, as though to drink from it, he deliberately spilled it on the ground as he said these words: "Far be it from me, O Lord, that I should drink the blood of the men who got this at the risk of their lives." The lives of his brave companions were far more valuable than the sweetness of that precious water.

Shall water ever become so precious that people will risk their lives in order to get it? Shall water ever be as precious as blood itself? Already it has been so. Already in history many have fought and killed to get water when there was not enough. Already in our time we know that transfusions of liquid are needed to keep blood flowing. The lifeline of clear fluid into the veins can be as valuable as blood itself.

When water becomes that precious, do we recognize that it is a gift from God? Only, I suppose, if we recognize that all things are gifts of God.

Another story from the Bible shows what a gift can be. It is the story of Hagar, driven from the tents of Abraham by the jealous demand of Sarah to whom she was slave.

Rising before dawn, says the storyteller of Genesis 21, Abraham gave to Hagar some bread and a skin of water. He put it on her shoulder and the woman with her son journeyed into the desert of Beer-sheba.

They journeyed until the skin of water was empty and dry. Then they stopped. Without water the woman knew that death was near. She laid her child under a bush to shelter him from the killing sun and walked a bowshot away to sit down and await their inevitable fate. As she sat there, she heard the child crying. But God heard the lad's crying too, says the storyteller, and a messenger of heaven called to Hagar the mother. "Pick up your lad," said the voice, "for he must become the father of a great nation." She did that, and as she held Ishmael in her arms, she looked up and saw a well of water. Quickly she ran to it, filled the empty water-skin, and put its nozzle to the lips of the thirsty boy. Life returned to her and her son. She learned to live there with him in the desert, and when he had grown, she found him a wife in Egypt. Today all Moslems look back to him as their forefather.

For those who live in the North, now is the beginning of winter. It is the time for snow, so why think of water except in the form of snowflakes? The beginning of winter is the time for rain in the land of the Bible. As the clouds pour the life-giving rain from above the people of that land have learned to pray and sing about water in lines like these:

> You have visited the earth with water,
> you make it abundantly rich.
> You water its furrows,
> you make the clouds pour,
> you soak it with showers
> and bless the new sprouts   (Ps. 65:10-11).

Whether it comes in showers or blowing through a December night, it is water and, in both ways, a gift of God. The coming of water is one of the comings of God. It is by such coming that God gives us life.

> Praise you for water in all its forms, for water in clouds, for water as dew on thirsty ground, for water as ice or snow or sea, because without it we could not live and with it we know you as giver of life while we drink.

13

Boaz the Redeemer

The story of Ruth is a Bethlehem story about redemption, the story of a family that almost died out. The only two people left in that family were Naomi, an elderly woman of that village, and Ruth her daughter-in-law from the neighboring but foreign land of Moab. Both were widows. If they died as widows, their property and the family line would be lost.

When she came to Bethlehem with her mother-in-law, Ruth made a vow of faith. "Where you go, I go," she said. "Where you dwell, I shall dwell. Your people shall be my people, your God shall be my God. Where you die I will die and there I will be buried" (Ruth 1:16-18).

And when they settled down in Bethlehem, Ruth went out in the grainfields to glean behind the harvesters with the poor folk of the village and the strangers. By chance she gleaned in the fields of a man named Boaz—which was fortunate, for Boaz was a near relative of her dead father-in-law, and in the custom of Bethlehem it was the obligation and duty of men to take care of their brother's family if he should die.

Boaz took notice of Ruth and treated her kindly. As the harvest season continued, he saw that she got an abundant share of the grain. When the season was over, the wise old mother-in-law, Naomi, advised Ruth to offer herself to Boaz. Her words were frank and clear: "Boaz is kin to us and tonight he shall be winnowing grain at the threshing floor. You take a bath and fancy yourself as finely as you can. Then go down to the threshing floor. Keep out of sight but watch the man. When he has eaten his meal and lies down for the night, then you go to where he is lying down. He will do the rest" (Ruth 3:2-4).

Ruth did as she was told. She went so far as to crawl under the blanket of Boaz to lie at his feet. With this she startled the man in the middle of his sleep. Boaz was awakened and quite surprised to see her there. But he was impressed and deeply moved by her offer. The very next day he cleared all the legal details, and Ruth became his wife. This made her a full-fledged citizen of Bethlehem. They had a son who carried on the line and the property of the family that Ruth had joined. More important than that, that son's grandson would be the mighty King David.

What Boaz did in the story we call *redemption*. Boaz redeemed Ruth and Naomi and the entire family line of his dead brother Elimelech. He did it by accepting Ruth and caring for her, by marrying her and taking care of his brother's property. But it went deeper than that, of course, for it began with the way that Boaz looked at Ruth. When he looked at her, he saw what she was worth. He saw her beauty and her strength and her bravery. "Everyone knows that you are a woman of character," he said to her when he first met her. Most of all, he believed that about her and honored her by becoming her husband. That is how he redeemed her.

In a way, we could say that Ruth redeemed Boaz as well. She

saw his value as a wealthy and respected man of Bethlehem. She knew that she could find no better husband than this. Boaz understood her redeeming love. That is why, on the very night when she offered herself to him at the threshing floor, he said to her, "Blessed of the Lord are you, my daughter. This act of kindness is greater than the first—even greater than your coming to Bethlehem with your mother-in-law. How good that you have chosen me rather than some other man."

What is it that happens when one human being redeems another? In how many ways can we do it? It starts by seeing how precious the other person is or can be. It ends by taking care of that other person in some way or other.

The people of ancient Israel had a law called the law of redemption. It was a way of caring for the needy or rescuing kinfolk from slavery. The basic law is found in Chapter 25 of the book of Leviticus: "If your brother becomes poor and sells part of his property, then his next of kin shall come and redeem what his brother has sold." It goes on to describe the details of such a purchase and the conditions that require its practice. Further along we see how the law could even affect a person, for we read this: "And if your brother becomes poor and cannot take care of himself with you, you shall take care of him."

With this law of redemption those people provided for each other. Family property was protected in this way. Widows and orphans and other needy persons were taken care of. This was regarded as God's law. It was God's will, they believed, that people should care for each other in this way. And when they practiced this law, people were saved by it—saved from poverty and need, from loneliness, and even from slavery and prison.

Think what it must have been like to be redeemed. When the relatives stepped in to help, the person could say, "I am worthwhile after all. They see that I deserve to be a member of this family. They see that I belong, that I count as a person."

Naomi, the mother-in-law of Ruth, spoke her thankful feelings by saying, "Blessed is he who has not forgotten to be kind to the living as well as the dead!" It made her feel good to be counted and valued. The coming of a redeemer for her and her family was like the coming of God himself.

Praise you for caring and for all those people who care for others, for hands that help another and ears that listen to troubles, and gifts that give honor and importance to all of your children, no matter how poor or distressed or lonely they be.

14

God Our Redeemer and Jesus Too

Thinking about things works best when we can picture them in our minds. We can think about a stone or a tree or a favorite toy very easily because we can make pictures about those things in our minds. But we can't picture God—which is why one of the commandments is about not making images of God.

In order to think about God we must think about what God does instead of what God looks like. God is known by what God does.

We can think of God as the Creator. That makes it easy. We live in the midst of God's creation and, therefore, all we have to think about God as Creator is to think about a sky full of stars, an ocean full of creatures, of the land so busy with bugs and birds and beasts—not to mention the trees and the grass.

The people who wrote the Bible liked to think about God as their Redeemer. They meant that God does things that are like a brother helping a brother in need. God finds what seems to be lost and makes it part of the family again. God takes things that seem to be dead and makes them live and grow. God has a way of making worthless things worthy, and that is what redemption is all about.

There is an entire psalm in the Bible that is about redemption. It starts like this:

> *"Give thanks to the Lord, for he is good!*
> *His brotherly-kindness is forever."*
> *So say the redeemed of the Lord,*
> *those he redeemed from the hand of oppression,*
> *gathered from the lands,*
> *from the east and the west,*
> *from the north and the south*   (Ps. 107:1-3).

As they looked at their own history, they recalled many times when God had spared their lives and carried them through. There were times when all hope was gone and the end seemed near. But strength came from somewhere, and they went on. As they looked back, they knew it was God who provided that strength and the way to more life. That was redemption.

God had redeemed them from slavery in Egypt. He had redeemed them from the desert, from enemies on every side, from plague and disease, and from invasions by mighty armies that nearly removed the names of Israel and Judah from the lists of the nations. One of their prophets was especially fond of thinking about those things. It gave him hope for the future that he spoke of in words like these:

> *Fear not, you worm named Jacob,*
> *you people of Israel!*
> *"I will help you," says the Lord.*

Your redeemer is the Holy One of Israel. . . .
He who created you, O Jacob,
he who favored you, O Israel,
"Fear not," says he, "for I have redeemed you.
I have called you by name. You are mine"

(Isa. 41:14; 43:1).

To say things like that was like saying, "God is your brother. God is your kinsman who looks after you." It helped them remember that God is in charge of life and of history. God was in charge of their story, and God is in charge of the story of all other people as well.

It is easy for us to forget that. It is easy for us to think that God is somewhere far, far away. So when we pray to God, we pray as though we are writing a letter to a faraway grandpa. "Dear God . . . " we begin, just as though we are writing a letter. But God is not far away. God the Creator is in the world creating new wonders every second of the day. God the Redeemer is giving new life and new hope every second of every day just as well. Someone steps on a blade of grass, crushing it beneath the heel of a shoe. God causes the blade of grass to stand up and grow again. A fledgling bird falls out of a nest. It should die, but God can make a bird like that grow despite all the odds. A terrible war rages, and hundreds of thousands of people are driven away from their homes. In the refugee camps they starve and waste from disease. "Surely they shall all die," we say, but somehow they live. They escape to the sea, and though many die, as many go on—on to another land where they start life all over again, even learning to speak a new language. All that is redemption.

The people who wrote the Bible knew much about redemption. They had experienced it many times. Their descendants, the Jews, know even more about it by now. Besides all that is in the Bible there are 2000 years more of being redeemed by God. Last of all, some were redeemed out of Hitler's holocaust which took six million of them. Early Christians, escaping persecution by the Roman government, learned a lot about redemption too. God as Redeemer is one of the big lessons of our tradition.

The psalm about redemption, Psalm 107, goes on with many lovely lines. "Some wandered in the desert, not finding a city to dwell in," it says. "Hungry and thirsty, their spirits were fainting. Then they cried to the Lord in their trouble and he freed them from their distress." And it goes on to speak about those who sat in darkness and gloom, living in prisons, about those who were sick from their sinful way and those who went to the sea in ships. Many were the kinds of folks in distress who came to know this great lesson: when God comes, he comes often as our Redeemer.

But it is not only God who can redeem. People can do it too. If a boy fixes the leg on an injured dog, the dog is redeemed by what the boy does. If a mother sews patches on an old pair of pants, the pants are redeemed.

A person can redeem another person by paying attention to that person—by loving, by caring, by helping in any way. Redeeming another person is what happens when we treat someone else as worth being with, worth talking to, or worth liking.

Jesus was a man who did that sort of thing. He went around the land he lived in redeeming others. Jesus, like Boaz, played the part of a brother. He had no money with which to redeem lost property as Boaz did. Nor could he afford to purchase the freedom of a slave. He simply did what he could with the nothing that he had. He dared and cared to be brother to many. At last he gave his life to redeem the world.

Jesus believed that all who desired the will of God were truly his brothers and sisters. He believed that any honest person in need was a neighbor deserving his help. It didn't really matter how closely he was related to the person in need. What mattered was that he was willing to be a neighbor, a friend and a brother, to those who were willing to allow him to help.

There were many who came to know Jesus because he redeemed them.

There was Mary, the woman of Magdala. "She's a crazy woman," her neighbors said. "She has seven devils in her." But Jesus treated her as a person to be respected, and she became one of his closest friends. He redeemed her with his love, and the demons left.

There was the daughter of Jairus, lying on the bed of death. "Get up, little girl," he said. The child came back to life, though to all those around her bed she seemed to be dead. By paying attention to that child he redeemed her. They counted her as dead; he saw her as alive, and she came to life.

There was Nathaniel. Just a man standing around, one could say. But at first introduction Jesus recognized the worth of the man. "Behold an Israelite in whom there is no guile," Jesus said. Nathaniel became a devoted disciple, a person with a new sense of honor.

There was Zacchaeus, the little man who was alone in his tree because as a collector of Roman taxes he was not popular in town. Jesus spotted him up in the tree. "Come on down," he said, "I must visit your house today." The Roman collaborator was redeemed by that call and that visit. It changed his life. He gave half of his goods to the poor and offered to pay back anyone he had cheated. When Jesus saw the man's willingness to change, he declared, "Today salvation has come to this house, for he is now also a son of Abraham. The Son of man came to seek and to save the lost."

It was in seeing the worth of those people that Jesus redeemed them. They were important to him, and when he treated them as important persons, they became important. That's what redemption is all about. The price he paid to redeem them was the attention that he gave them. That redemption was the coming of God to their lives. Jesus was that kind of coming of God to one person after another.

But there was also a way in which Jesus redeemed the whole nation of his people. We find words about it in the beginning parts of the Gospel According to Luke. There is the hymn of Zechariah, first of all—the words that the old man spoke after his long silence before the naming of his infant son John: "Blessed is the Lord God of Israel, for he has visited and redeemed his people."

The words of Mary at the discovery of being pregnant with Jesus are words about God lifting the lowly. Those words are a hymn of redemption:

> *My spirit rejoices in God my Savior*
> *for he has regarded the lowliness of his servant.*
> *From henceforth all generations will call me blessed!*
> *He has put down the mighty*
> *and exalted those of low degree.*
> *He has filled the hungry with good things*
> *and sent the rich away empty* (Luke 1:46-48, 53).

As Luke wrote the story of Jesus for us, he understood it to be a story about redemption. One at a time, Jesus redeemed the people he met, and living his life as he lived it, Jesus the Jew of Galilee redeemed the entire tradition of his people Israel. He was their light and their glory.

> *Praise you for things that Jesus did to raise the lowly and pick up the fallen, for the love that looked toward people and the care of his healing hands, for the power that came through his words and his deed, and for all redeeming power that comes to us in his story and in your world of wonders.*

15

The Candle of the Shepherds

The third candle is known as the Candle of the Shepherds. Why shepherds? Because shepherds were there at Bethlehem the night that Jesus was born. Because Bethlehem was a village of shepherds. Because shepherds were what the Hebrews were from the beginning. Shepherding was their way of life. Talk about shepherds fills the Bible from one end to another. From the Bible we have even learned to say:

> *The Lord is my shepherd; I shall not want.*
> *He lets me lie down in green pastures;*
> *he leads me beside the quiet waters and brings back my*
> *breath.*
> *He leads me along the right paths for his own name's*
> *sake* (Ps. 23:1-3).

To say, "The Lord is my shepherd," is to step back in time and place to a land of many hills where shepherds could be seen all over the country, tending their flocks of goats and sheep. To say, "The Lord is my shepherd," is to pretend that we are goats and sheep. How else could the word *my* have any meaning? If the Lord is my shepherd, I must be like a goat or a sheep.

There is nothing romantic about shepherds and sheep, even though that is the way we probably see it. If we were to make the same kind of confession of faith to suit our times and trades, we would have to begin with a line like one of the following:

> *The Lord is my mechanic.*
> *The Lord is my bus driver.*
> *The Lord is my doctor.*
> *The Lord is my welfare worker.*
> *The Lord is my keeper.*

Because the ancient Hebrews were shepherding people, it was sensible for them to say, "The Lord is my shepherd." It was an ordinary sort of thing to say. One couldn't find a more ordinary way to talk about God, nor a less flattering way to talk about themselves. As surely as we say something about God, we end up saying something about ourselves, and the Hebrews were confessing that they were like sheep.

They did not mean, of course, that God really is a shepherd. That kind of talking is what we call *metaphor*. They used metaphors in order to talk about what they couldn't really understand. They were not able to understand God any better than we can. That is why they used metaphors in their speech, and that is why we must.

We could say, for example, "The Lord is my conscience." That would be a metaphor. God isn't really my conscience, and the voice of my conscience is not really God's voice. God is far bigger than that. Yet I could mean to say that God guides and protects me in the way that my conscience guides and protects me.

The truth of the matter is that we cannot successfully compare God to anything that is small enough for our minds to grasp. That is why we are forbidden to make images of God, I suppose. A great Hebrew prophet said these things in a magnificent way:

> *"To whom will you compare me*
> *that I should be like him?" says the Lord.*
> *Lift your eyes high and look: who created these?*
> *He brings their multitudes out by number,*
> *calling them all by name. . . .*
> *Not one is ever missing*   (Isa. 40:25-26).
> *As the heavens are higher than earth,*
> *so my ways are higher than your ways,*
> *my thoughts than your thoughts*   (Isa. 55:9).

The truth that we must begin with is this: there isn't anything we can name that is anything like God.

God is a word to itself. We can try with words to talk about what God does, saying such things as, "The Lord is my shepherd, my light, my king, my fortress." (Those are the phrases used by psalmists of old.) But all words fail to define God. God is beyond definition and too big for words. God is so big that all other things we know of, including every star in every galaxy and all of that put together at once, are smaller than God.

And yet God may be within it all or in any small part of it as truly as God can surround it all. God is mystery. Mysteries are not to be understood. But mysteries must be believed and trusted, for if we do not believe in the mystery, we shall know no greater security in life than our own wits or our own strength. If we believe only in things we can understand, we shall never believe in anything bigger than our own brains.

To believe in God is to believe in the truth that is greater than all truths we can know or understand. It is to believe in what we must believe in because we have no choice.

No choice. No choice but to breathe the air that creation provides. No choice but to drink the waters he created. No choice but to eat and to live from the hands of the Creator. No choice but to rely on the One that makes all worlds and this world, the One who creates me and all that exists, who gives and still preserves for me body and soul and all that I am, who daily, abundantly provides for all of my needs.

It is true, then, to say that the Lord is my shepherd. Who else provides the green pastures in which we can lie if we will? Who else provides the water that restores our lives? Who else provides safe ways and places to live? Who else wards off evil by filling my system with cells and substances that fight off disease? To whom else do I owe thanks that I am alive this day and as long as I live?

I must accept this care, this gift called life, and to accept it is to believe. And if I accept it and thus believe, why not go the rest of the way and confess it? Why not sing in grateful praise? Why not say something childlike and simple like this: "The Lord is my shepherd. He comes to me as a shepherd comes to his sheep."

Praise you for feeding and leading, for guiding, protecting and keeping us all alive each day, for being the One on whom all depend and in your one-ness forcing us all to be sheep together as though we are all really one big flock.

16

Shepherds and Shepherding in the Bible

From the beginning of the story the Hebrew people were shepherds. Abraham, Isaac, Jacob, Jacob's sons—all of them were keepers of sheep. (Only Joseph was an exception; he was the great farmer of Egypt.) Moses, after fleeing the land of the Pharaohs, kept flocks for Jethro, the priest of Midian, in the desert.

When they were taken away from their land by the armies of Babylon, they had to stop being shepherds in order to till the farms of Nebuchadnezzar. But when survivors returned to the hills of their homeland, many of them turned again to the keeping of sheep. The men who were guarding their sheep on Bethlehem's hills in the reign of King Herod were men of an ancient tradition.

All those connected with Bethlehem were also connected

with the raising and caring of flocks. King David was the shepherd son of the shepherd Jesse. The woman named Tamar, David's ancestor, gave birth to her son Perez by enticing Judah as he journeyed to a gathering of men for the shearing of sheep. Bethlehem was surrounded by hills where flocks moved in ribbons like hair tumbling from the head to the shoulders of a woman.

No wonder, then, that the Bible has so much about shepherds, and no wonder that God is sometimes described as shepherd. No wonder that Jesus spoke of shepherds and shepherding. No wonder that shepherds were the first to know of his birth.

Had the Savior come from another culture, our images of speech would have been of another kind—of ships and sea lanes, perhaps, of horses on Anatolian plains and of those who kept them, of caribou on the tundra and the hardy ways of Lapland, of herds of cattle and tall Masai warriors on the eastern African plains. But Christendom's Savior was a Hebrew, and that cannot be altered. He was a Jew, a descendant of the son of Jacob named Judah. He was the offspring of shepherding people.

"Salvation comes from the Jews," Jesus said one day to a Samaritan woman. That is a basic teaching of the Christian faith. The Christian thing to say about God is that God came as a Jew.

At the beginning, all Christians were Jews. Before the name *Christian* was invented—and the book of Acts says that occurred in Antioch of Syria (Acts 11:26)—Christians called themselves "followers of the way," "disciples of Jesus" or simply "the poor." Almost all of them were Jewish. They were Jews who first took Jesus as Messiah. They were Jews who went forth as his apostles. The gospel they took to the gentile world was a Jewish gospel. The very words in which the gospel was first spoken were the words of Hebrew tradition. They were the words of a shepherding people.

Does this mean that God could reveal himself only in this way, only through those people? Does it mean that Jews had special talents to be prophetic? Does it mean that those people were better than all other people? Or does it mean, as one clever person once said, that God always wanted to be a Jew?

The answer to all these questions is most likely *no*. God is surely much bigger than one human language or one human tradition. God is, after all, the God of all peoples.

Yet the people of Israel had one special task that set them apart as different. They had the task of proclaiming the one-ness of God wherever they might be. *"Shema' yisra-el, edonai elohenu, adonai echad"* is how they learned to say it. "Hear, O Israel, the Lord your God is Lord alone," is what that means. Wherever they have lived in this world they have testified to the truth of that.

Jesus the Jew inherited that task. He prayed it as a Jew when he prayed these words: "I pray, Holy Father, that they may be one even as we are one." One people called Jews, one God called Our Father, one people on earth who are all God's children—these were the things that Jesus prayed for. He was a Jew, a faithful Jew who proclaimed that God is one. And he made himself one with all people. That is what brings us together, and that is what makes for peace in this world. By Jesus we are made one with God and one with each other. The big word for that is the word *reconciliation*. It means that all things are brought together by what Jesus was and believed and did.

Jesus said, "I am the good shepherd." Did he say that of him-self, or was he speaking, as a prophet speaks, for God? A few lines before it, in the gospel of John, we hear him saying, "I am the door of the sheepfold." He thought of himself as one who sat at the gateway, watching as sheep come in from the fields to gather in the fold. He stood at the entrance where flocks came together from their travels in order to become one larger flock. He was like a door through which they enter.

Early Christians prayed a prayer about people gathering to-gether from many nations. It was prayed in the Communion service, after the sharing of the bread and the wine:

Before all things we give thee thanks that thou art power-ful. Thine is the glory forever and ever. Remember thy church, Lord, to deliver it from all evil and to perfect it in thy love. Gather it together from the four winds, even the church which has been sanctified, into thy kingdom which thou has prepared for it. Thine is the power and the glory forever and ever.

—From *The Teaching of the Apostles*

That reminds us of a prayer Jesus prayed. "I have other sheep, that are not of this fold," he said. "I must bring them also, and they will heed my voice. So there shall be one flock, one shepherd" (John 10:16 RSV).

There is, then, one God and one true shepherd. That makes us all one people, no matter how different we are in any way. The message came through one people and then through one person. But this message of shepherding one large flock is a message for all the world.

Praise you for flocks—for flocks of all colors and ways from all sorts of places on earth, but most especially for this, that no matter how different we are, we are still and truly just one large flock in a world that has you as only one shepherd.

17

Bad Shepherds and the Good Shepherd

We hear so much about good shepherds and the Good Shepherd that sometimes we forget whether there ever were any bad shepherds. A prophet named Ezekiel informs us that there were:

> The word of the Lord came to me saying, "Son of man, prophesy against the shepherds of Israel, prophesy and say to them . . . Ho! Shepherds of Israel who have been feeding yourselves! Should not shepherds feed the sheep? You eat the fat, you clothe yourselves with the wool, you slaughter the fatlings; but you do not feed the sheep. The weak you have not strengthened, the sick you have not healed, the crippled you have not bound up, the strayed you have not brought back, the lost you have not

sought, and with force and harshness you have ruled them. So they were scattered, because there was no shepherd, and they became food for all the wild beasts. My sheep were scattered, they wandered over all the mountains and on every high hill. My sheep were scattered over all the face of the earth with no one to search or seek for them

(Ezek. 34:1-6 RSV).

Ezekiel was speaking, of course, about the leaders of Israel and Judah. They thought of their leaders as shepherds. Ezekiel dared to say that they were bad shepherds. Why? Because they had ruled with their own selfish gain in mind. They were not concerned about the people. They were bad shepherds who cared only to fleece the sheep.

Had they been good shepherds, how would they have ruled? A good shepherd was a man who became so concerned for his sheep that he would risk his own life to save them. To the good shepherd the sheep came first. No matter that he is raising them for gain—for profit from the wool, the milk, the hides or the meat. Engrossed in the business of shepherding, he behaves as though safety of the sheep is the end and purpose of it all. He gives himself for the sheep.

Ezekiel went on to say that because the shepherds had failed, the Lord himself would come to replace them:

Thus says the Lord God: Behold, I, I myself will search for my sheep. I will seek them out. I will bring them out from the peoples and gather them from the countries. I will bring them back to their land. I will feed them on the mountains of Israel, by the fountains and in the settled places. I will feed them good pasture. On the mountain heights of Israel shall be their pasture. There they shall lie in good grazing land. I myself will be shepherd of my sheep. I will seek the lost and bring back the strayed. I will bind up the crippled and strengthen the weak

(from 34:11-16).

When human leaders have failed, God steps in and takes care of his people. "Would that God had been shepherd all along," we might say. "Would that we never had human shepherds!"

We think about nations and governments in our day. "Bad shepherds we still have," we might say. There are still leaders who lead for their own sake rather than for the sake of the people. How often the leaders lead the sheep into war instead of to peace! Our country has already seen two great world wars, and we know that a third could happen. Any of the many little wars could become the war that would end us all. There are enough bad shepherds to make it happen no matter how much the people don't want it. "Would that God would step in!" we might say. "Would that God would get rid of all governments and rule us himself by his own laws!"

That would mean going back to living in the lap of nature. It would mean being primitive again. It would mean living like wild animals out in the wilderness. They live by God's laws alone. (The domestic beasts, like cattle and dogs and cats, live by the rules of their human masters.) What is life like for them? It is to live by the instincts that the Creator planted within them and eat from the supply of whatever wild foods are available.

Long ago we chose to leave that way behind us. We don't remember it, of course, because our ancestors made the decision for us. It was the day that we decided to raise our food in cages and fields in place of being foragers and hunters. It was the day we invented the village and the day we invented the city. It was the day we learned how to throw pots on a wheel and the day we learned to forge iron. It was the day we appointed a court of justice and asked for a king. Step by step, again and again, we decided we wanted to govern ourselves. We told God we wanted to have our own shepherds and be our own shepherds.

And God let us do it. God allows us to govern ourselves and God allows us to make almost as big a mess of the world as we will. God allows us to kill and make war. God allows us to ruin

our natural environment. God allows one people to destroy another, with machine guns or in chambers of poison gas. God
allows us to be incredibly foolish or evil.

When does God get tired of it all? When does God step in to
be our shepherd? At the very first sign of failure? Most certainly
not. When he hears the cries of suffering? No, not necessarily.
God allows that to go on and on. Only when we have finished
our mess, perhaps. Only when we have done all the damage we
can do and our taste for plunder and war has gone dry. Perhaps
then is when God takes over.

When the wars are ended and the bodies of the soldiers are
buried, then God comes and covers them gently with grass and
decks the fields with bright poppies. When the bombing is done
and the miners have finished blasting the mountain, then the
Creator sends seeds that will turn our cities and tailings back
into wilderness again. Thousands of cities and pits of the past
have been covered that way.

When Ezekiel lived, a great war had ended and the prisoners
of war still lived as captives. After a time, the captors grew tired
of watching. They were conquered by others, and the prisoners
were free to return to their homeland. Under God's guidance
alone they went back. For a moment in history they were simply
people, God's people. God led them. God fed them. God kept
them alive. He dealt with his people as he deals with the birds
of the air and the flowers of the field. He restored them.

Could God be our shepherd as he was shepherd to them? Only
if we are willing to be God's sheep. Only if we are willing to be
simply people and not proudly American, German, English, or
Japanese. Only if we are willing to be governed by God's laws,
to submit to nature and stop forcing her to give us all that our
greed demands. Only if we truly prefer God's peace to the kind
of security that depends on armies and missiles and tanks and
military secrets. If we are willing to accept such terms, then, God
might govern whatever survives.

God could come as Good Shepherd, but only if we are willing
to be like sheep.

Praise you for patience that outlasts all of our foolish and evil ways, for being our God in silence as well as in power, for leaving us alone in wisdom that we do not understand, but most of all for being our hope in the midst of our own stupid and foolish behavior.

18

Tender Shepherd, Bless Thy Lamb

There is a picture of Jesus we love most dearly. It is Jesus as shepherd, walking through a valley with a lamb in his arms. Jesus is robed, and his eyes are most tender. We easily find ourselves feeling that each of us might be the little lost lamb that he carries so gently.

Behind the picture is a parable about a shepherd who left 99 sheep in the fold to go out and look for one lamb that was lost. It was told in order to tell us that God is like that, and the Man who told it proved he believed it by acting like that himself. "I came to seek and to save that which is lost," he said.

Behind the parable is a little poem in the Book of Isaiah:

> *He shall feed his flock like a shepherd*
> *and gather the lambs with his arms.*

He shall carry them in his bosom
and gently lead those that have young   (Isa. 40:11).

In the chapter that has these lovely lines about God as tender shepherd, we are told that God is coming with might. "The Lord God comes with might," we read in the very verse preceding. "How strange," we might say, "that one so mighty can be so tender." But perhaps that's the way it had to be. For the people who first heard these words, it was a message to announce a time of peace and ease from the burdens that had oppressed them for many long years. They had been prisoners of war. The mighty God was releasing them, and that was a tender thing. The mighty God brought their enemies down to defeat, but for them that was gentle care.

We think of those people who endured the prison camps of the wars of our time. How relieved they must have been on the day they were freed by liberating armies! The medical care and the abundance of food that was given them starting that day must have seemed too good to be true. The quality called mercy must have been precious indeed.

So it was for the people who first heard the words we read from the Book of Isaiah. They had grown accustomed to bondage and exile. The announcement that God would now lead them gently and carry the lambs must have been downright delicious.

But how did God do it? Did he personally make an appearance? No. The prophet knew clearly how God had come. He had come in the coming of Cyrus the Great, the liberating conqueror of Persia. It was King Cyrus who set the captives free and allowed them to go to their homelands.

For the prisoners of the concentration camps of World War II the coming of the Allied Armies was the coming of God. The gentle hands of an English soldier or the gift of a Russian's loaf of bread were the gifts of the coming God. It is always like that. God helps one human through another. God uses us to care for each other.

Moses was the coming of God to the Hebrew slaves in Egypt. David was God's coming as shepherd to the tribes around Hebron when tyrannical Philistines ruled the place. Judas Maccabaeus was the coming of God to the Jews who were tired of cruel Greeks. Martin Luther was the coming of God to Germans who were sick of Roman domination.

There is this curious teaching in the Bible that God comes through the hands of our neighbors to shepherd us gently. Jesus showed us how it works between one person and another. He taught that a cup of cold water, a cloak for a naked back, bread for the hungry, and a visit to the lonely were God's way of bringing relief. It is as though God is in each of us and as though in our serving each other God serves both us and himself. This is the very order of creation. One part serves another. The rain serves the earth with life-giving water, but the earth alone can give back the moisture that makes the clouds. It is as one part serves another that the whole world is made healthy. Nature always works this way, and human societies work best when they do too.

It is all so simple that perhaps only children can understand it well. When a mother tucks a child into bed and helps the child sing the little song, "Jesus, tender shepherd hear me, bless thy little lamb tonight," it is the mother who is truly being the shepherd for God and for Jesus. She serves as God's arms for the child.

When brother helps sister and sister helps brother, they are the caring of God for each other. When a friend helps a friend or, still more impressively, when a stranger helps a person in need, that is God coming as tender shepherd. Jesus taught us that love is to do such deeds, and that is what he meant when he said we must love our enemies too. To love is to give tender care.

It is in this way that Jesus himself came to us. He was God coming as tender shepherd. He had an eye for the lost and the lowly. He had the gift of healing in his hands. Those who were touched by his hands knew that they had been touched by God.

It is not that Jesus was God in the all-encompassing grandeur of the Creator of worlds. He was not God in the formless magnificence that is beyond our comprehension. He was, rather, the smallness of a man. But he came with the kindness and tender mercy that saves us from despair. He touched us with God's own touch. He was mighty, but he was gentle in using that power to cheer and to heal.

Praise you for pictures of comfort, for acts of kindness wherever they are done, for hands that are gentle, for words of mercy, for strength that is used to free people from prisons, to heal the sick and bind up the wounded, and for all gentle ways that make us rejoice.

19

We Like Sheep
Who Go Astray

It is not very smart, in a way, to talk about the comings of God. Why should we talk about the coming of One who is here? He is here and there and everywhere. Being the Creator, God is in all creation. Without his presence the whole show would come to an end. God never left his creation, and God never leaves us. He is in all, above all, beneath all. Isn't it silly to speak of his coming when he has never gone?

There is a psalm that thinks such thoughts for us:

> *O Lord, you have searched me and known me.*
> *You know when I sit, when I rise.*
> *You understand what I think.*
> *You stand in front and behind*
> *and press your hand down from above.*

Such knowledge is far beyond me.
It is deep; I cannot understand it.
Where could I go to escape?
Where could I hide from your presence?
If I climb to the skies you are there.
If I lie down in death, there also.
Could I flee on the wings of the dawn
and camp far beyond the ocean,
even there your presence would follow.
Your strong arm would grasp me.
If I say, "Let the darkness enshroud me!
Let the daylight around me be night!"
I find that the dark cannot daunt you,
that night seems bright as the day
and darkness like light.
It was you who formed my organs
and clothed me in the womb of my mother.
I confess it: you are marvelous.
The things that you do are amazing.
You have known me from the beginning   (Ps. 139:5-14).

So does God ever leave us? Not really. As surely as we are alive, God is near. God is what keeps us alive. But, from time to time, it can seem that God leaves us. Because we can fail to notice his presence, God can seem to be far away. And if we should go on supposing that God is not near, we might end up supposing that there is no such thing as God anyhow. It is then that we need to read such a psalm as the one we just read.

It is only because of our failure to see or hear or sense God's presence that we need to talk about Advent, which is the coming of God. It makes us think of what we have forgotten, and when, for the first time in a long time, we think about God's presence, it seems as though God has decided to come again.

We read about this unnoticed presence of God in the opening chapter of the Gospel According to John: "he was in the world yet the world did not know him. . . . He came to his own

but his own did not receive him. . . . He was from the beginning . . . and to those who did receive him he gave power to
become children of God." To those who hadn't seen him before, he seemed to come as though for the first time or as though
he had never come before.

"All we like sheep have gone astray," says the prophet in the
Book of Isaiah. Yet the shepherd was watching, and the shepherd was there. Only our foolishness turns us away so that we
do not see the shepherd. Yet the shepherd continues to shepherd until our foolishness is gone and we notice that he is there.
He will allow us to get into trouble. He allows us to suffer that
we might turn. But when we turn he is there.

As with all good shepherds, the shepherd we know as God
does not stand still. He does not merely sit and watch. As surely
as sheep are on the move, the shepherd moves too—even more
than the sheep. For when we are lost and in a strange place, we
discover that he, the shepherd, got there before us.

God is not still. God is not immovable, like a pillar or a rock.
God is energy. God is always coming and always going. God, at
one moment, can seem to be behind us, but then we look around
and discover that he is ahead. Yet always, whether we know it
or not, he is in our midst. Like electricity or the incredible movement of atoms or the exploding of a star, God is never still.

Our ancestors in the faith had a name for God that recognized all this movement. *Yahweh,* they called him. *Yahweh* is a
verb, not a noun. It means "he makes happen." They knew that
God is That which makes other things happen. They knew he
was there in all that happens—in life and death, in the passing
of seasons. They knew that God was always coming and always
going and never doing nothing.

To experience Advent is to be aware of all that moving. It is
to discover that we can always look for the appearance of God.
It is to be surprised, again and again, by God's coming and to
learn to live for the sake of that surprise. It is to be like the
shepherds on Bethlehem's hills, faithfully watching yet suddenly
surprised by the sudden light and the sound of angels singing.

This combination of waiting and surprise is the very delight of life. Without the waiting there is no faith, but without the surprises there is no joy in our faith.

Praise you for coming and praise you for going, and for all the moving and for our little comings and goings within the movement of your ceaseless moving. Praise you for glimpses that tell us that you are there and always here among us.

20

Like a Lamb Led to the Slaughter

Like it or not, sooner or later, we all must die. It's a sober and serious thing, and sometimes it makes us afraid. Just thinking about it can hurt. Even when it comes in its time, to someone old and ready to die, death can cause pain. Those who gather around to mourn, feel that pain as they feel the loss.

More terrible than death in its time is the violent and sudden death that wrenches life from an unwilling body and that body from its circle of friends. When that happens, we feel terror and shock as well as the pain of the loss. Such death can linger as nightmares that keep us awake many nights after.

Most terrible of all, perhaps, is the slow and painful death of lingering illness or cruel torture. Such death is endured again and again as each day of waiting drags on. It draws forth amazing strength from our frail flesh and leaves an exhaustion that demands as many days of healing as there were days of pain.

Yet death is only a part of life. As inevitable as the rain or the setting of the sun, it comes to us all. To be born is to die. To live is to die. We know this no matter how much we may put it out of mind. The only thing we don't know is when it shall happen —though we may well know when it is near. A terminal illness or extreme age can assure us that death is near, and in such cases death may become a dear friend.

When we tell the story of Jesus, we must always tell the story of his death—not merely because he had to die as surely as we all have to die, but because he chose to die at an early age and because of the way he died.

At the beginning of his brief career, the cleansing prophet of the Jordan valley had pointed his finger at him and said, "Behold the lamb of God who takes away the sin of the world." Here was not the shepherd. Here was one of the sheep—one like us and one of us. Here was a lamb to be led to the slaughter. Like us all he had to die, but, because he accepted it in a way that we can't, he decided when and where and why to die.

We could very well do the same, I suppose. *As long as I have to die,* we might say to ourselves, *I may as well die for something worthwhile and choose my own death.* Others than Jesus have done that from time to time in the human story.

"He died for us," we say. What does that mean? Does that mean that he became one with us all, that he chose to die simply because he knew we must die?

"He died for our sin," we say. What does that mean? Because we often enough die as a result of the foolish mistakes we make, did he die because of our foolish mistakes? There were Jews in his day who were ready to die foolishly in a war against Rome. Some of them would have made Jesus their king. So he died as their king, with KING OF THE JEWS written over his head. Was he dying for their sins? Not many years later, thousands of them went to war against Rome and died for that cause.

Jesus taught us that there is only one who can take our lives from us. That one is God, the giver of life who takes all life back to where it came from. Perhaps that is why he could face death so bravely. He believed that in death he would meet his Father. He had showed us first how God comes to us. Now he would show us how we come to God.

And how do we come to God? As naked as how we came from him. Like Jesus, we must leave our garments to those gathered round. We enter the tomb as we came from the womb —naked. Those two events bring us together in nakedness: the event called death and the event called birth.

Christmas is about the birth event. It is the feast of the babe in the manger. It is about God coming in the guise of the infant and the wonder of newborn life. Yet death lurks all too near. As we speak of the birth of the Christ, we must anticipate his strange and early death. The carols of Christmas give way all too soon to the lamentations of Lent.

It is all a rhythm, this coming and going. God comes to us, we come to God. God comes and comes and comes. There is birth and rebirth. There is resurrection. We sometimes sing about that in one of the Christmas carols: "O Holy Child of Bethlehem, . . . be born in us today." It is true, is it not? The Christ does rise, and the Christ is reborn, and God does come to us millions of times and in millions of ways. When we celebrate Christmas, we do not celebrate only one coming. We celebrate all comings, and we celebrate the belief that God comes again and again. As we celebrate the birth of the Baby, we celebrate the gift and the source of all life.

Death is not the end. Death is not the greatest fact. Were such a thing so, there would be no life and no world. There would be only nothing. Life is the end of it all, as it is the beginning. Life appeared in Bethlehem's manger, the very life of God among us. Let us celebrate that with joy and abandon.

Praise you for death and dying because they are only parts of the rhythm of living. Praise you for life that is always stronger than death, because all things now living prove to us that life is stronger than death and that death is only a meeting with life and with you, who are Lord and giver of life.

21

In Turning, Turning
We Come Out Right

Every day now for many days we have talked of the coming of God. If we believe these things, we know that God comes to us in a multitude of ways—in the speech of nature, in things that happen, in Jesus, and in the lives of people who do things for each other. So many ways are the comings of God that we might feel surrounded or even smothered by his comings.

When we were very little, life with mother and father was like that for us. We played in our cribs and whenever we needed the slightest thing, mother or father was there. If we cried because our diaper was wet, mother came with a dry one. If our crying said "I am hungry now," mother was there with her breast or father was there with a bottle. If ever we were lonely, one or both of them would appear to entertain us. Indeed, they didn't wait for us to become lonely. Most likely they came when they felt like coming, to tickle our toes or, if we were sleeping, just to stand there and look at us.

As we grew up, that changed a bit. Mothers and fathers still came, but the older we grew the more we had to yell to get them to come. There even came a time when mother and father grew tired of coming. Not only tired, but eager to tell us that we wouldn't grow up unless we began doing things for ourselves. But even as late as our teens, when we needed most anything from a button to a misplaced school book, our cry would go up. "Ma!" we would shout down the stairwell. Somehow, in a sudden moment of need, we expected mother to come at our call.

It's like that with God, and yet it is not like that. Like parents when we were young, God comes even when he is not needed and not asked. Unlike parents, however, there never comes a day when God stops coming. The biggest difference is this, however: God's coming is always in disguise. It is like a thief in the night, as Jesus once said. Because God cannot be seen, we never see him coming in the obvious way that a parent comes when the baby cries. God's coming is in those disguises we have been hearing about. It's a subtle kind of coming —always happening, always to be seen, but only noticed by those who have eyes to see and ears to hear, as Jesus and the prophets put it.

In yesterday's meditation we thought about dying as our way of coming to God. Apart from that, it seems as though all the coming is God's—God's coming to us. It is no wonder, perhaps, that Martin Luther left us a Catechism in which we find these words: *"I believe that I cannot by my own reason or strength believe in Jesus Christ my Lord or come to him."* Martin Luther knew that the coming was one way—from God to us.

But is that totally true? Are there not many times in which I come to God? Are there not times when the sheep truly come to the shepherd?

There seem to be times when we do the coming. There seem to be times when the sheep hear the voice of the shepherd and come. There are times when we yearn for the presence of God and long to come to him. There are even times when God seems to be absent and we cry out, "My God, my God, why have you forsaken me?" "How long, O Lord, will you stay far away?" "As a deer pants for the waterbrook, so longs my soul for you, O God." (All those lines are found in the Psalms.)

If such longings are not a desire to come to God, then what are they? Do we not actually move toward God when we pray such words? And when we sense God's presence after such longings, can we not say that we have found God? Have we not come to him? Yes, so it seems. But no, not really.

What we find when we come to God is that God never really went away. What we discover is the presence that was hidden by our fears, our doubts, or the dullness of our perception. What we discover is that we were not so much coming as merely turning to see the One who was always there.

Turning is a big word in the Bible. "Turn to me and live" is a line we find in the prophets. "Turn from your wicked ways," is another. "Turn to me and be saved, all you ends of the earth," is a precious line from Chapter 45 of Isaiah.

Within such lines is the simple teaching that God is the source of all life and each moment of life. In turning to God we turn to that source and find there all that can give us new hope and new courage. To turn to God is to live again, for it is a turning to Life. To turn to God is to receive those things that help us go on through difficult days: forgiveness, energy, courage.

Sometimes we fear to turn because of our guilty feelings. We fear that in turning we shall be punished or even condemned. Like a little boy who has stolen some cookies and is too scared to look into the eyes of his mother, we fear the wrath of God when we feel guilty for our mistakes. But if we dare to turn in spite of our fears, we discover that God is forgiving. "Let the wicked forsake his way," said a prophet of old. "Let him return to the Lord, that he may have mercy on him, and to our God, for he will abundantly pardon" (Isa. 55:7-8 RSV). And a psalmist, who had discovered the secret, said it this way, "I will teach transgressors your ways, and sinners will turn to you" (Ps. 51:13).

In turning to God we are often surprised, especially when something inside us condemns us. The surprise is forgiveness. God permits us to live in spite of our sin. Even Cain, who killed his brother Abel, was permitted to live after the murder. (Only one thing changed for him. He then had to live for the brother he killed, as well as for himself.)

Sometimes we use the word *repent* in place of the simpler word, *turn*. Perhaps this is not a good idea. Why not? Because we have learned to use the word *repent* as a threat.

Repent is one of the words of Advent. "Bear fruit of repentance," said John, the prophet of Advent. But his message was followed by the baptism of repentance, and baptism means *washing*. It was the washing that permitted the fruit of repentance. Washing made it possible. Washing was good news, which we call gospel.

When the gospel was spoken by Jesus, it was spoken with the word *turn* or *repent* in it. Jesus said, "The Kingdom of God is near. Turn (or repent) and believe in the good news" (Matt. 4:17). To turn and believe was not a threat. It was a promise and an announcement.

In a simple old American hymn we find these important lines:

> *To turn, turn shall be our delight,*
> *for in turning, turning we come out right.*

Indeed we do, for in turning we behold the everlasting coming of God.

> *Praise you for words and all other signs that cause us to turn, for things that stop us, that force us to look and to listen, for things that scare us or hurt us in order to turn us that we might look to you and learn, once again, to live.*

22

The Candle
of the Angels

When people think about angels, they often think of fat little people with wings, naked and yet without sex. They picture angels as children who fly, children who have died and gone to the Lord, who serve him as messengers now, perhaps. Angels are usually invisible, folks think. But when they are seen they must look something like that.

We picture angels in our minds the way they are pictured in paintings and sculptures of old cathedrals of Europe. We see their pictures in books, we are told such are angels, and so we imagine that that's how they look. Because that's the way it is, some other folks say that angels are purely in our imagination.

When wise men of the Middle Ages wrote about angels, they said angels are usually invisible, like God. As they described them, they sound a good bit like the particles and energies that are discussed by physics teachers and other scientists. Indeed, if we should ever read what they had to say about angels and then read the things that scientists say, we might decide that the two were talking about the same thing.

Unfortunately, none of this helps us understand what the word *angel* means in the Bible.

The word itself means *messenger*. It is a Greek word which, in one of its forms was pronounced *angelos*. In the Hebrew language, which is the language of the Old Testament, the word is pronounced *mal-ak*. One of the books of the Bible has that name in its title, the Book of *Malachi*. *Malachi* is not the name of the prophet who left us those words. The word means "my messenger" and it was used as the title for that scroll because that is what the scroll is about. As for its author, no one knows his name.

So in thinking about this Candle of the Angels, we shall be thinking about messengers—messengers who were or are the coming of God and messengers who carried the message of God's coming. There is much about them in the Bible.

The messengers we think about first are those who appear in the second chapter of the Gospel According to Luke. First there was one, and then the one became a multitude of the heavenly host.

Right there we have a clue about how angels appear. The *heavenly host* is the biblical way of talking about the stars in the sky. The stars were God's army or host. And why not think of the stars that way? They are as organized and disciplined as ever an army could be. They obey the orders of their general, the Creator himself, as perfectly as ever one can obey. And they keep watch over earth all night, and even all day when we do not see them.

The idea that the stars are an army of messengers of God is early in our tradition. They are the signs that tell us the seasons, according to the opening chapter of the book of Genesis. They tell us where we are in God's time.

There are lines in Psalm 19 that tell us of the message these messengers bear at all times: "The heavens declare God's glory," we read. "The skies display his handiwork. Each day pours forth a speech; each night proclaims some knowledge." And what is their message? Their message is the glory of God. It fits, then, that the song of the angels on Christmas Eve is "Glory to God in the Highest!" That is eternally the sum of what the stars and planets have to say. But they sing it; they don't merely say it. There is a music of the stars to which some people have learned to tune in.

The message of Luke's angels went on, of course, beyond that. It was a message of peace on earth among men of good will—men who know God's good will—or blessing for the earth.

Peace is one of the big words of the Bible. The Hebrew word for it is *shalom,* a word that means all good things rolled into one: health, prosperity, fruitfulness, and happiness. *Shalom* is the opposite of conflict and war and all that happens in time of war. *Shalom* is the biggest wordful of sound we know in any language. It is, in fact, the very substance of God's "good will." The announcement of God's great gospel blessing is "Peace on earth." It is the message that passes all other messages in goodness. It is like the sun rising with healing in its wings (or rays), and the book of God's messenger, Malachi, says that this victorious sun rises for those who respect God's name.

Throughout this week we shall think about messengers—not just messengers in general, but the messengers who brought the gospel of peace.

> *Praise you for peace and all that makes peace, for all that is good and healthy and living, and for the armies of heaven above that sing the message of peace and every little messenger on earth who carries that message to us.*

23

Angels Unawares

Once in a while people still talk of "angels unawares." When something wonderful happens and we don't know why it happened or when someone does a kind deed for us that we do not deserve, we say that the person who did it was an angel unawares. The ancient Greeks used to think that way about their gods. They believed that one should welcome every stranger at the door because a stranger might be a god in disguise. Our Hebrew ancestors, believing in one God instead of many, believed that a stranger could be a messenger of God—an angel unawares.

Our favorite biblical story about this sort of thing, I think, is the story of the three visitors who came to Abraham at the oaks of Mamre. "The Lord appeared to him by the oaks of

Mamre," says Chapter 18 of Genesis, "as he sat at the door of his tent in the heat of the day."

Abraham lifted his eyes to look. Behold, three men were standing before him. When he saw them, he ran to meet them and humbly bowed to the ground. "My lords," said he, "if it please you, do not pass on from your servant. Allow a bit of water to be drawn and wash your feet. Rest yourselves beneath the tree. I will fetch some bread so that you can sustain yourselves after your journey— for it is to your servant you have travelled, is it not."
"Yes, do as you have spoken."
Abraham hastened to the tent, to Sarah, and said, "Quickly! Take three measures of fine flour. Knead it and make loaves." Then he ran to the cattle, took a young steer, good and tender, and gave it to the herdsman, who hastened to prepare it. He took butter and milk, and when the steer was ready, he set it all before them. He stood by beneath the tree while they ate.

This was the way that hospitality was properly performed in the ancient world of our biblical ancestors. They believed, after all, that any visitor could be a messenger of God. As it turned out, these men were. They were angels with a double message. One was the happy message that Sarah, the childless old wife of the desert chief, would have a son and finally learn to laugh. The other was an announcement of doom. It was the message that Sodom and Gomorrah were doomed to destruction by the natural causes of God.

Angels can bring either good news or bad. The message can be a surprise of such joy that one can scarcely believe it. Sarah laughed when she heard what they had to say, because she believed it could not be. (God and his messenger had the last laugh. That's why, when the child was born, they named him *Isaac,* which means "he is laughing.")

Or the message can be so dreadful that we, like Abraham, might well get down on our knees to beg for God's mercy. Life is like that. God's world is like that. There can be laughter and joy at the news of God's coming, but there can be tragedy too. There are times for birth, for planting, for keeping. There are also times for death, for harvesting, and for losing. (The third chapter of Ecclesiastes tells us more about that.)

How do we accept such opposites in life? How do we accept the angels of God when the angel may bear either bad news or good tidings—or both at once, as these messengers did? Abraham has shown us the way.

To begin with, one welcomes the guest at the door. No matter what his or her appearance, we must welcome that guest. That person may be rich and well-fed or one of the hungry and poor. If the person at our door is hungry or thirsty or naked and we provide what he or she needs, then what we have done was done for God. "Inasmuch as you have done it to the least of these my brethren," says the Judge, "you have done it to me" (Matt. 25:40). We must treat each stranger or guest as though that person could be our Lord in disguise. That is the code of behavior by which we shall be judged, according to Jesus.

If the guest is an angel with good news, how shall we respond? Perhaps, like Sarah, we shall respond with what is in our heart. If the years have made us bitter, we may doubt the good news. We may laugh out of turn—only to have the laughter turned to joy later on. How we respond to good news is beyond our control. It merely reveals what is in us. But once we have given vent to those feelings, we may as well believe what we hear. Why cheat ourselves of possible joy when joy comes to us? Why not drink it to the full and make the most of all that God can give? All good news, which is gospel, is meant to be enjoyed.

What if the news is bad? Again, our reactions will reveal what is in us. Self-pity will overwhelm some of us. Some will seek the first possible escape. Some will resign themselves to what must be. Abraham dared to protest because of his concern for the victims.

Lord, will you destroy the righteous together with the wicked? Suppose there be fifty righteous people in the city. Will you destroy? Will you not spare the place for the sake of fifty righteous people in it? It would be terrible for you to do such a thing—to destroy the righteous together with the wicked. How terrible of you! Should the Judge of the world not practice justice? (Gen. 18:23-25).

Abraham argued and bargained until it was conceded that for ten righteous persons God would spare Sodom. But there were not that many and so the city was destroyed. (To this day Jewish people say that the world or any place in it is spared only when there are at least ten righteous men in it.)

What good did it do for Abraham to plead with God and argue against him? Sodom and Gomorrah were destroyed all the same. The God who sends rain on the fields of the just and the unjust without discrimination also sends fire without discrimination. Both wrath and mercy are experienced by the good and the evil alike. God's justice is not like ours. His ways are not our ways, and our sense of justice can well rebel against God's.

But Abraham, the model of faith, pleaded for the sake of Lot and Lot's family. What else should a man of faith do? A person of faith is also a person of compassion. Faith relies upon God for life and for mercy. The person of faith knows that others have the right to rely on him in the same way. Therefore he is compassionate. He pleads for brothers and sisters who are suffering or about to suffer.

So how should we act when angels come to our door? With hospitality first. Then, when their message has been delivered, we must react as we are. We must be honest. What we are is revealed in our honest reaction. It is best when the news is good and we can be surprised by joy. But if not, if the news is ever bad news, may we be as courageous and compassionate as Abraham, the father of the faithful.

Praise you for all who come in disguises to teach us, to warn us, to surprise us with gospel, to give us those mo-

ments in which we find out who we are and what we are like and how much we need the strength of faith as we meet those whom you send our way.

24

He Will
Send His Angel

The Book of Malachi, the last book of the Old Testament, has an unknown author. Not knowing who wrote its prophetic words, the scribes simply headed it with the word *malachi,* which means "my angel." The word comes from the third chapter where we find this well-known Advent text:

> *Behold me sending my messenger. He shall prepare the way before me. Suddenly he enters his temple, the Lord whom you seek, and the messenger of the covenant who is your delight—behold he comes. Who can endure the day of his coming? Who can stand when he appears? For he is like a refiner's fire, like fuller's caustic. He shall sit and refine like a purifier of silver. He shall purify Levi's descendants and refine them like gold or silver.*

Then they shall bring proper offerings to the Lord. Then the offering of Judah and Jerusalem will be as pleasing as in years of old (Mal. 3:1-4).

These words became important in the New Testament. They were used to explain the ministry of John the Baptizer. John was concerned with such things, with purification and righteousness. He preached about turning and presenting God with righteous lives as an offering.

And Jesus picked up where John left off. John pleaded for turning and change in the wilderness. Jesus went into the temple itself and overturned tables as he denounced the people in charge. His words were strong: "This house should be a house of prayer, but you have made it a den of thieves!" (Luke 19:45).

But there are things we should know before we can understand the actions and words of both John and Jesus. There is something to know about priests and the tribe of Levi.

Priests were people who worked in the temple. When worshipers came with animals to be offered, the priests were the butchers who butchered the beasts, draining the blood into basins, carving the carcass, and burning the fatty parts on the altar. The priests were the men who saw that incense burned day and night on the incense altar. The priests prayed for the people and then turned and blessed them with the great benediction of Aaron: "The Lord bless you and keep you; the Lord make his face shine upon you and be gracious to you; the Lord smile upon you and give you peace."

Levites were the men who assisted the priests. The priests were Levites too, of course, for all of them together were descendants of Levi, but the name *Levite* was usually used for the more ordinary members of the clan. The Levites were the musicians, the assistants, and the janitors who took care of the temple and all the celebrations that happened there.

And the temple? The temple was a huge stone building with grand courts around it. There were courts for the women, courts for the men, and courts where only the Levites and priests were allowed. Only the priests were allowed in the temple itself, and in its most secret place, the Holy of Holies, only the high priest entered.

In more ancient times, when there was no temple, the Levites and priests did their work in a giant tent. The people came out of the wilderness with that tent, and then it was set up at Shiloh, a town in the hills of Ephraim. It was destroyed by Philistines in the times of Samuel and Saul.

The temple in Jerusalem was built in the time of King Solomon. It was a grand affair, and it stood on its hill called Mount Zion for over 300 years. Then Judah was conquered, and Jerusalem was destroyed. The temple was leveled to the ground. The people of Jerusalem were carried away as prisoners of war. About 70 years later many of the captives returned, and in the years 520-515 B.C. the temple was built again. From that time on, it was the priests and the rest of the tribe of Levi who were its ministering servants.

They had little choice about it, to tell the truth. From earliest times their tribe was chosen to be the priestly tribe. They could not own much land. They had no way to make a living other than to work in the temple. It was no wonder, perhaps, that they tired of the job and became halfhearted about it. Through thick and thin they had to serve. Even when all the rest of the Israelites wandered from the way, the priests and Levites were expected to serve in the temple. The rituals went on even when believers no longer believed. No wonder, then, that the priests themselves would lose faith.

The Book of Malachi is a book about their loss of faith. In a halfhearted way the priests had been offering scurvy animals and polluted food at the altar. They had grown tired of requiring the best of the flock and the finest of flour and the choicest oil of the olive. If the people were unwilling to put their hearts into the rituals of worship, why should the priests be loyal and faithful? Could the priests be better than the people they represented?

There were those who believed that the priests should honor God even if the people should fail and forget. Why? Because the priests did not only represent the people. They represented God as well. And because God was faithful no matter how unfaithful the people might be, the priests should be faithful too.

The priests represented the God who is Father of all. All the people of Israel were supposed to bear witness to that. They were supposed to recite the words of the great *shema: "Hear, O Israel, the Lord our God is Lord alone."* If Israel should fail to repeat those words, how would the people of earth know that there is only one God, who is Father of all?

For the priests it was even more important. If all others failed, they should not. So when even they failed, a prophet spoke of a messenger who would come to purify the sons of Levi. He spoke of a righteous teacher who would teach them the meaning of the rituals they were required to perform. He would purge them and cleanse them with his teaching. He would be like fire, like the purifying fire of the rising sun, like the sun whose rays bring healing to earth each day.

The messenger who was predicted was a messenger of judgment and correction. He would be stern. He would demand that the priests and the Levites do their jobs with devotion. But underneath his garments of judgment would be the garments of mercy. The purpose of his judgment, after all, was to heal and to save.

In Advent we think of John the Baptizer as such a messenger —and Jesus too. John scolded the priests and Levites in the same way they were scolded in the Book of Malachi. Jesus visited the temple and cleansed it by kicking out those who didn't belong there with their business. Like surgeons who cut in order to heal, their anger and indignation was for a good purpose. They came to heal and to save.

Praise you for stern and terrible words that demand the cleanliness and the honesty we need in order to be healthy and whole, for words that tell us when we are weak or wayward or failing to do our task, and for the gracious forgiveness that lets us leave the failures behind and try once again to do what we should.

25

How Beautiful
Are the Feet

Long ago, in the days when the Bible was being written, long before telephones or postal service, messages were carried by messengers. They were runners who could run long distances without stopping, and they had to be brave because sometimes bandits would try to stop them along the way and take whatever they had. The finest messengers were those who worked for the armies or the government. The long-distance race called the Marathon reminds us of a runner who carried a message of victory more than 20 miles across the plain of Marathon to the people of Athens in ancient Greece. (His name was Pheidippides, and he ran so hard and fast that after he delivered his message he fell dead.)

Messengers who brought bad news, like the defeat of an army in battle, sometimes came in with dirt on their heads, wailing and lamenting. Messengers with good news came leaping and smiling.

In Chapter 52 of Isaiah there is a poem about a messenger who had good news:

> *How beautiful on the mountain*
> *are the feet of him who brings good news,*
> *who announces peace,*
> *who reports good things,*
> *who announces salvation,*
> *who says to Zion, "Your God rules!"*

Beautiful? Why? Because for a long time there had been trouble and oppression. The people had lived in a foreign land as prisoners of war. There had been defeat. There had been marching away to Babylon. Those of the first generation were almost all dead and gone. Only a few remained who had been little children on the day they were led out of Judah as captives. For nearly two generations they had waited for an end to it all. Beautiful indeed were the feet of him who could bring them good tidings of peace!

What had happened was this: a great king named Cyrus had conquered the people who held the Jews as captives. Under Cyrus, the King of Persia, it was now decreed that they could go back to their homeland. They were to be free again.

Peace is most precious to those who have experienced war or wandering and trouble. The angel of peace is most welcome when people have yearned for peace and suffered in their yearning. When a prisoner has sat in a cell for countless days and lifts his eyes to behold the feet of one who stands at the door of his cell and sees that the door is open and hears the words, "You are free to go"—that is when the messenger's feet are beautiful feet.

The Hebrew word that we translate as *peace* is a word too big to translate. It is a word that means all good things rolled into one. It can mean good health, good times, prosperity, friendship, security, rest, celebration, or all of those things together. Its opposite is war because war is the breakdown or disappearance of all those good things.

The Hebrews believed that peace was a gift of God. Sometimes that gift was called *salvation,* which also means an end to war or an end to suffering. Like all the gifts of God, peace or salvation are gifts that grow and abide. Peace is produced by the same energies that produce God's gifts of nature around us. Peace is created, like earth and all that is in it. The prophet who spoke the words about the beautiful feet of the messenger of peace also spoke beautiful words about God's creating ways. He spoke about God as one

> *who created the heavens and stretched them out,*
> *who spread out the earth and its produce,*
> *who gives breath to the people upon it,*
> *breath of life to those who walk there*   (Isa. 42:5).

He spoke of peace as something like water in the desert, fountains in the valleys and rivers on the heights. Best of all for many of us, he spoke of forgiveness as God's gift of peace. Forgiveness is healing and without such healing the memories of war and disaster can disturb the enjoyment of peace.

> *"Comfort, comfort my people,"*
> *says your God.*
> *"Speak tenderly to Jerusalem*
> *and call out to her*
> *that her sin is pardoned,*
> *that her time of war is finished"*   (Isa. 40:1-2).
> *I, I am he who blots out your transgressions*
> *for my own sake. I will not remember your sins*
>   (Isa. 43:25).

The message of peace is a much-needed message—not that the energies of peace are lacking. To the contrary, the energies of peace are constantly there. Without them earth would perish. It is, rather, a case of what kinds of messages make the news. As we read newspapers and magazines or listen to TV reports, we find that the messages of war and disaster make more news than the things that make for peace. Our modern messengers seem to be more in tune to evil than good—or perhaps it's what readers and listeners most love to read and to hear. Too few are the angels of peace.

And who are those angels of peace? They are those who know the good news of growth and life that goes on despite all our foolish ways. They are those who know the power of sunshine and water and bread and forgiveness. They are those who live tuned to the energies of God's world and, because of that, are filled with the hope that our tired old societies desperately need.

At times we can read their messages on a printed page. At rarer times we hear their words on the radio waves. Most often they come simply, on human feet, for these are the angels who still know the need of the human touch. They come as one person to others to talk about good things—about life and love and friendship. They are angels, these people. They are angels of peace, messengers of good news. They come with comfort and understanding. They come for God as all angels of God and their coming is like the coming of God himself. For whoever brings peace brings God's own gift.

Praise you for beautiful feet, for feet that run in their haste to bring good tidings and feet that come gently with comforting words that end our sorrow, and feet that dance as they come to cheer us, and feet that come boldly to challenge the doers of evil and rescue the prisoners of earth from oppression. Praise you for feet of all angels and for the gospel of peace!

26

He Makes the Winds
His Messengers

Who, among us, would ever think that the winds are angels of God? In the Bible it is quite natural to speak that way. *Angel* means *messenger,* and to say that the winds are angels is to say they are messengers of God.

When we think of God's world, we must think of all those things in nature that can give us messages about God or from God. And when we begin to think that way, we can understand how the winds or any other part of creation can be angels of God.

Angels can come in many forms in the Bible. Or, to put it another way, we could say that the Almighty uses whatever or whomever he will when he needs a messenger. Mortal men and women have served as messengers and for that we call them prophets or prophetesses. A donkey served as an angel to the prophet Balaam, according to the story in Numbers 22–24. The phenomena of nature are messengers in a big way according to the Bible, as in these lines from a psalm:

> *He makes the winds his messengers*
> *and bolts of fire his servants*   (Ps. 104:4).

How can the winds be messengers in God's kingdom? We feel the wind and hear its sounds, and these sensations tell us things. In the northern parts of the earth the winds of March and April bring the first announcement of spring, while the winds of November promise the snow. There are winds of the sea that tell of fair weather or foul. There are dreaded winds of the desert that threaten through scorching and cutting sand. There are winds for every part of the planet, and each wind has a message. There is a speech of wind that some people come to know and understand. Such speech is truly speech of God. The winds are messengers of creation and the Creator.

In ancient times the wind was more than a mere messenger of the seasons. People thought that the wind was the energy of God himself. They spoke of the Wind of God or the Wind of Holiness as a way of talking about how God gets around in our world. Sometimes we translate those phrases as *Spirit of God* or *Holy Spirit.* The word *spirit* is the old Latin word for *breath* or *wind.* This means that we could also say *Breath of God* or *Holy Breath.* Let us recall some places in the Bible where these phrases are used.

The opening lines of the Bible are about creation, and the wind, the breath of God, is what does it. "Wind of God was hovering over the face of the waters," it says. Then comes the speech of God that causes light and all the other wonderful things of creation. The wind is like a messenger there, announcing all those things that are about to happen.

When the Israelites came out of Egypt, that was an event of God's creation. The drying of the waters of the Shallow Sea of Reeds was accomplished by the east wind blowing, according to the book of Exodus and the Psalms. Ever after that, the east wind was considered a special wind in the hands of God.

The creation of human beings was by the breath or wind of God. "The Lord God breathed into his nostrils the breath of life," we read in the second chapter of Genesis, "and Adam became a living creature." The breath of God as our source of life is a precious thought we find in other places in the Bible as well:

> *You take their breath and they die*
> *and go back to the dust they came from.*
> *Yet you send back the breath and create,*
> *renewing the face of the earth*   (Ps. 104:29-30).

> *The dust returns to the earth as it was,*
> *and the breath returns to God who gave it*   (Eccles. 12:7).

We could say that the breath of God is an angel of life.

Special gifts of life are credited to the breath of God—or the Spirit of God, as we usually say it—rare gifts of bravery such as the gifts of Gideon or Samson or Saul, the artistic gift of Bezalel, the man who designed the Tent of Meeting, or the gift of prophetic speech. The conception of Jesus in Mary's womb was a gift of God's breath as well. "Holy breath will come upon you and power of the Highest will shadow you," said another kind of messenger (Luke 1:35).

What does it mean to say that Jesus was conceived by the Holy Spirit—by the "Breath of God"? It means that, like Adam, he was and is primeval. He is one who comes from the beginning. His very conception and birth were a fresh new creation by God. When Mary was "visited" by the Holy Breath of God, the source of all life became the source of life within her. And when he was born, according to John, we beheld his glory as the glory of the specially-begotten son of God (John 1:14).

As Luke went on to tell the story of Jesus, he used the word *spirit*—that is, *breath* or *wind*—to talk about what made Jesus do what he did. Translating the word as *breath* makes some of the lines come out like this: "Jesus, full of Holy Breath, re-

turned from the Jordan and was led by the Breath for forty days
in the wilderness" (Luke 4:1-2). "Jesus returned in the power
of the Breath into Galilee" (4:14). "And he came to Nazareth,
where he had been brought up; and he went to the synagogue,
as his custom was on the sabbath day. And he stood up to read;
and there was given to him the book of the prophet Isaiah. He
opened the book and found the place where it was written:
'The Breath of the Lord is upon me' " (4:16-18).

All of life fits together. Everything about life is connected to
everything else. It is like a single piece of cloth, no matter how
many the patterns or colors. The wind and the breath are the
same. The wind of God, the breath of God, the spirit of God—
all these are one and the same. They are ways of talking about
life and where all life comes from. To say that the spirit or
breath is of God is to say that life is of God and that breath is
one of the ways in which it comes to us. It is, indeed, an angel
of life.

One of the things said about Jesus is something like this.
We read it in the opening chapter of the Gospel According to
John:

> *In him was life, and the life was the light of men.*
> *The light shines in the darkness,*
> *and the darkness has not overcome it* (John 1:4-5).

In the 1960s we used to sing a song that had these lines in it:
"The answer, my friend, is blowin' in the wind." There was
ancient truth in those modern words. More truth, perhaps, than
intended. The biblical poet who wrote the lines about the
winds being messengers of God would have understood that
line well. The winds are the way in which God comes from the
beginning—coming to create the earth and renew it, coming
with prophetic words to prophetic lips, coming to bring life
and all the gifts of life.

Once there were disciples gathered in an upper room to wait
for the coming. The wind began to blow, and they were filled

by that wind or breath of God. It turned them into messengers of God, and they became angels to the world.

> *Praise you for mysteries such as the winds that blow unseen over our world, blowing gently or strongly, low on the earth or high in the stratosphere, and for the breath that fills all creatures and each of us, because this is all the gift of your coming and we wait to be filled by that breath.*

27

The Angels
Who Came in Dreams

From as far back as we humans can remember we have experienced dreams in the night, all kind of dreams—frightening dreams we have learned to call nightmares and dreams so deliciously nice that we hate to see them end. Our dreams can be bizarre and outlandish, or they can be so realistic that we find ourselves wondering if those things really happened.

We don't make as much of our dreams as we used to. That is all for the better, perhaps, for we need to be reasonable in order to live wisely. Dreams are usually too irrational to give us much clear guidance.

Yet it may still be that a dream can be a message for some and from time to time. There are biblical stories about the appearance of angels in dreams with messages of importance and comfort.

I think, for example, of Zechariah the prophet. He lived at a time of little things, a time of little hopes and little expectations. His people were subject to the mightiest political power of the times. They had freedom of worship, but they paid their taxes to a foreign nation called Persia. They were not a happy lot, for there was little to make them happy other than the blessed fact that they were surviving. Making a living was about all they could manage, and that was grim business for some.

They looked at their leaders, Joshua the priest and Zerubbabel the governor appointed by Persia, and they saw nothing of pride for themselves, nothing to make them optimistic. Joshua was dressed in dirty old robes. Zerubbabel was only a puppet of the Persian king. How could they be more than half-hearted about their existence?

But the Lord came to Zechariah in a dream. He came as a man with a measuring tape to measure Jerusalem for building expansion. "This will be a great city," said the man. "It will overflow its walls for the multitude of people and animals in it" (Zech. 2:4).

Then he looked at the priest in his shabby robes. An accuser, a "satan," was taunting him for his shabbiness. "The Lord rebuke you, you satan," said the angel. "This man is a brand plucked from the fire" (3:2). Then he gave new garments to the priest and put a clean turban on his head and said to him, "Thus says the Lord, if you walk in my ways and keep my commands, you shall have charge of my courts. . . . I will remove the guilt of this land in a single day and each of you will invite his neighbor to sit beneath his vine and his fig tree" (3:7-10).

That angel said more, but in all that he said he brought hope to those people. Zechariah learned the importance of little things and of seeing much in what is little. He was able to speak courage to his people because of the messenger who came to him in his dream.

In another age of hard times, angels appeared in the dreams of Daniel. The Greek kings of Syria had been oppressing the

Jews, demanding that they forsake the ways of their fathers. Finally things became so bad that the temple itself was desecrated by the despot who called himself Antiochus Epiphanes. It was a time when the mighty oppressed the weak.

The angels that appeared in Daniel's dreams assured those oppressed people that the saints of the Most High would prevail. The mighty king would fall from power in the midst of his own boasting. All cruel kingdoms would cease, and a humble Son of Man would rule for God in a kingdom that is forever. Those angels were also angels of gospel.

And the angels that appear in the Gospel According to Luke are messengers of good news as well.

One came to a priest whose name happened to be the same as the prophet of earlier times, the priest Zechariah. His message, according to Luke 1, was this: "Your wife shall have joy and gladness. She shall bear a son and you shall call him John. He shall turn many to the Lord their God." Another angel came to the virgin Mary to say, "Hail, favored one! The Lord is with you. . . . You shall conceive in your womb and bear a son and you shall name him Jesus. He shall be great. He shall be called the Son of the Most High" (Luke 1:28-32). According to Matthew, an angel came in a dream to Joseph, telling him to take his wife without fear, because her pregnancy was a work of the breath of God.

Those who visited the tomb of the crucified son of Mary saw a young man—or two young men—standing there in the garments of death, the white robes that signify death in the Jewish tradition. But their message was not a message of death. "He is risen," they said. That was their message: they were angels of joy. Their words broke the darkness of grief.

Often in life we despair. Discouraging things can lead us into such depression that our path of life seems to be entering a lengthy cave that will only become darker as we proceed. At such times we stand in need of hope. And what is the shape of hope when it comes?

Sometimes hope comes in the form of a friend who touches

us with a strong and gentle hand. Sometimes it comes as the good news that times have changed. Sometimes hope takes the form of a new way, a path of turning that leads to light.

Sometimes, at times when nothing is quite ready to happen but the waiting has been too long to wait any longer, hope may take the form of a visitor who comes in a dream to speak good news in advance of its coming. The message fills us with delight. "Can it be true," we say, "or am I just dreaming?" We awaken to find that we were, indeed, dreaming. Yet the hope created by the dream remains. We walk with lighter step and greater security than we did on the day before. We look to the future for further signs that will promise fulfillment of the dream. We work with that dream in mind. Then one day we realize that what we saw or heard in the dream has now become real. The vision has been fulfilled and we know, therefore, that it was true. God came in the night and he, the Lord of all darkness to whom the darkness is as day, instructed my mind in the night. In the midst of my sleep my Creator was with me as much as in my waking. He sent his angels to me, to be with me in darkness as much as I know the light. The hope abides. I can live and walk with a firmer step.

Praise you for all your comings, those that are clear to the light of day and those that are secret, the comings that are wrapped in the mystery of night. Praise you for dreams that speak warning and dreams that speak courage and for all the messengers of your mercy that appear and disappear but leave their messages with us.

28

We Hear the Christmas Angels

The angels most familiar to Christians are the angels of Bethlehem. Luke tells it like this:

> *And an angel of the Lord appeared to them, and the glory of the Lord shone around them, and they were filled with fear. The angel said to them. "Be not afraid, for behold, I bring you good news." And suddenly there was with the angel a multitude of the heavenly host praising God and saying, "Glory to God in the highest!"*
>
> (Luke 2:9-13).

What was the form of the angel who spoke? What did he look like? And who were the heavenly host?

All the way back in the biblical tradition the "heavenly host" is a way of describing the stars on high. *Host* means "army," and the Israelites thought that the stars were the army of God.

One section of the poem about Deborah, the woman who saved her people from the Canaanites in the 12th century B.C., has these lines:

> *The kings came, they fought,*
> *the kings of Canaan fought*
> *at Taanach, by the waters of Megiddo,*
> *but they got no spoil of silver.*
> *From heaven fought the stars,*
> *from their courses they fought against Sisera,*
> *and the river Kishon swept them away*   (Judg. 5:19-21).

The Canaanites lost the battle that day, not merely because of the bravery and skill of Israelite leaders and men, but because God's army was against them. The very stars of heaven joined the battle as torrents of rain flooded the Kishon river and stranded the chariots of Sisera.

Lord of hosts is a phrase so common in the Old Testament that we meet it a few hundred times. It means *Lord of armies,* and the armies it means are the stars of the sky. The phrase is especially common in the books of the prophets, but it is in one prophetic passage that we know it best:

> *In the year that king Uzziah died, I saw the Lord sitting upon a throne, high and exalted. His skirts filled the temple. Seraphim were standing before him . . . and one called to another and said, "Holy, holy, holy is the Lord of hosts. The fullness of all the earth is his glory"*
> (Isa. 6:1-3).

Sometimes I wonder if people understand what they mean when they chant the phrase "Lord of hosts" on a Sunday morning. Do they know that the words encompass the universe and connect the glory of earth with the glory of the stars? Or that the earth, which is the glory of God, is also one of the stars in God's army?

Our horizons tend to be limited to our own personal lives. We don't usually look beyond our own business when we think of the world. When we are children, we don't look far beyond the places where we play and go to school. When we are adults, we don't look beyond where we work or take our vacations. But if we say it with understanding, the saying of "Lord of hosts" makes those horizons disappear into the infinity of the stars.

The chemical components of a star and a human being are similar, I have been told. A living star displays the colossal grandeur of greatness and size in God's world. A human being shows God's cleverness. Yet both we and the stars are of the same stuff, and all are one in God's creation. We and the stars and everything on our planet are all tied together in God's great scheme.

Ancient Egyptians considered that the stars were the souls of departed persons. They may have been wrong—and yet right in knowing that we and the stars are connected not only by being of the same atomic components, but still more because we and they are made by the same Creator.

We like to think that heaven is another place, a place beyond us. Sometimes we like to think that earth is a cursed place of exile. We need to think that both have God's glory. The distances of space and the earth we live on are both in God's "hand." "The heavens declare the glory of God," we read in Psalm 8, but in this passage from the Book of Isaiah we read that "the fulness of earth is God's glory." Even this planet, where we all live, is glorious in the sight of God. The glory of the stars is near and here.

Perhaps that is the vision that the shepherds of Bethlehem saw on the Christmas night. An angel spoke, and suddenly they saw the heavenly host as they had never seen it before. The announcement of Messiah coming caused those Jews to hear the heavens singing, as the very stars proclaimed the glory of God and peace on earth.

What does it take for us to hear that singing or see that glory

—or to know the possibility of peace on our planet? Does it take the appearance of an angel? What was the appearance of the angel that night over Bethlehem? Was it a seraph with six great wings? Such would likely have been called a seraph and not an angel. Was it a mortal messenger wandering over the hills that night? Or was it, perhaps, one star—one star brighter than the rest that spoke the message?

Whatever the appearance of the angel, the message they heard connected heaven and earth that night. It taught us to hearken to the singing of the stars and to know that God comes in grandeur at the very same moment as he comes in the smallest and humblest way.

The coming of a baby and the birth of a star are two things of the same order in God's creation. The stars are the armies of his kingdom, but the babes are the first in faith, and out of the mouths of such babes God brings forth wisdom.

> *You, whose glory above the heavens is chanted*
> *by the mouths of babes and infants. . . .*
> *When I look at your heavens,*
> *the work of your fingers,*
> *the moon and the stars which you have established,*
> *what is man that you notice him,*
> *son of man that you care for him?*   (Ps. 8:1-5).

Who are we that we should be noticed? Yet the Creator does care enough to come to us.

> *Praise you for coming, for coming, for coming and being*
> *among us in your many mysterious ways and yet always*
> *above us and ruling your worlds as though from on high*
> *where we see your glorious armies marching forth on*
> *parade each night unto the next night and where, if we*
> *will, we can hear the singing of all creation as they and*
> *the earth sing your praise, your praise, your praise forever*
> *and ever.*